Training Your Shih Tzu

Joan Hustace Walker

BARRON'S

About the Author

Joan Hustace Walker is a member of the Dog Writer's Association of America (DWAA) and The Authors Guild. The author of 15 books and hundreds of articles, Joan has been nominated for 27 national awards, and received the DWAA's coveted Maxwell Award six times, including the award for the 2006 Best Single Breed Book. Joan has been active in conformation, obedience, performance events, and rescue at various levels of participation for the past 30+ years. She trained the #1 Whippet and #1 Hound in obedience when she was just 13 years old, and showed successfully in Junior Showmanship and in the breed ring. She currently serves as chauffeur for her daughter, Grace, as she competes with her Havanese in the breed ring and in Juniors.

All inquiries should be addressed to:
Barron's Educational Series, Inc.
250 Wireless Boulevard
Hauppauge, NY 11788
www.barronseduc.com

ISBN-13: 978-0-7641-4109-6
ISBN-10: 0-7641-4109-0

Library of Congress Catalog Card No. 2008025882

Library of Congress Cataloging-in-Publication Data
Walker, Joan Hustace, 1962–
    Training your shih tzu / Joan Walker.
        p. cm.
    Includes index.
    ISBN-13: 978-0-7641-4109-6
    ISBN-10: 0-7641-4109-0
    1. Shih tzu — Training. I. Title.

SF429.S64W35 2009
636.76—dc22   2008025882

Printed in China
9 8 7 6 5 4 3 2 1

Acknowledgments

This book would not be possible without the kind and generous help of Barb Pennington and Carlene Snyder, who freely shared their years of experience raising and training Shih Tzu with me. Also, a special thanks to Rich and Linda Garrison, the Viola family, and my daughter, Grace. I'd be remiss not to give a special thanks to Gigi and Chewie, but I have a feeling they'd prefer some garlic chicken.

Cover Credits

Front cover: Jean Fogle; Back cover: Tara Darling; Inside front cover: Tara Darling; Inside back cover: Jean Fogle.

Photo Credits

Joan Balzarini: page 105; Kent Dannen: pages 5, 7, 33, 35, 41 top and bottom, 47, 48, 50, 63, 64, 85, 93 top and bottom, 110, 111, 117, 123, 125, 127, 128, and 132; Tara Darling: pages 4, 76 bottom, 99, 107, and 143; Cheryl A. Ertelt: pages 16, 51, 55, and 77; Jean Fogle: pages 11, 23, 31, 69 bottom, 76 top, 78, 81, 91, 120, 129, 130, and 138; Isabelle Francais: pages 12, 14, 36, and 95; Karen Hudson: page 71; Curtis Hustace: pages 2, 26, 27, 38, 72, 82 bottom, 89, and 121; Daniel Johnson: page 58; Paulette Johnson: pages x, 6, 13, 15, 19, 21, 24, 39, 43, 45, 57, 61, 67, 83, 113, and 136; Pets by Paulette: pages viii, 53, 60, 73, 92, 103, 106, 118, 133, 134, and 137; Shutterstock: pages 8, 46, and 79; Margery Squier: pages 3, 22, 34, 37, 62, 74, 97, 100, 119, 126, 139, and 146; Joan Hustace Walker: pages 40, 49, 69 top, 82 top, 84 left and right, 87 all, 88, 90 all, 96 left and right, 101 left and right, 104 all, 109, and 114 all.

Important Note

This book tells the reader how to train a Shih Tzu. The author and the publisher consider it important to point out that the advice given in the book is meant primarily for dogs of excellent physical health and good character.

Anyone who adopts a fully grown dog should be aware that the animal has already formed its basic impressions of human beings. There are dogs that as a result of bad experiences with humans behave in an unnatural manner or may even bite. Only people that have experience with dogs should take in such an animal.

Even well-behaved and carefully supervised dogs sometimes do damage to someone else's property or cause accidents. It is, therefore, in the owner's interest to be adequately insured against such eventualities, and we strongly urge all dog owners to purchase a liability policy that covers their dog.

Contents

Socialization 32

Developing a Dog-friendly Shih Tzu 44

Habituation: In and Out of the Home 56

Basic Training Principles 68

Five Basic Commands 80

Fun Activities with Your Shih Tzu 128

Useful Addresses and Literature 140

Index 147

Preface

There is no question that the Shih Tzu is one of the most popular breeds in the country today. The breed has it all: beauty, intelligence, loyalty, and that little bit of spunk that makes this dog 100 percent "Shih Tzu." If there ever was a dog bred to be a constant companion, the Shih Tzu is it.

However, no dog, no matter how bright and loving, comes prewired to be a perfectly behaved, well-mannered house pet. He doesn't know where it's okay to relieve himself, how to walk nicely on a leash, or that he'll get more pats and loves if he sits calmly rather than jump up and do his Shih Tzu dance. Ready and willing as the Shih Tzu is to be the perfect pet, he requires training.

The purpose of this book is not to create the next obedience champion or top-ranked agility dog (though you might discover while working with your dog that he is capable of many great things). The real intention is to provide some insight into the way a Shih Tzu learns, unravel some of the mysteries of why he does the things that he does, and teach owners how to shape desired behaviors with positive, reward-based training methods.

Training Your Shih Tzu is not intended to be the "end all" gospel of training; it is a guide to training. Though most Shih Tzu possess certain breed characteristics that make them similar to train, each Shih Tzu has a unique personality with individual likes and dislikes, abilities and challenges.

Because of this, your Shih Tzu may respond better to some training approaches than others. For this reason, I've detailed several approaches and strategies for training different commands and behaviors. Experiment a little. As you work with your Shih Tzu, you'll discover what works best for him.

Most importantly, it is hoped that *Training Your Shih Tzu* will help you to keep an open mind about new ways to train your dog. Training methods are constantly evolving. Positive, reward-based training is the approach of choice but, every day, people are coming up with more and more innovative ways to teach behaviors and solve problems. Keep your eyes and ears open. Read training articles. You may be the next person to come up with a different way to teach a Shih Tzu a new skill.

Always remember that if it's not fun, it's not (effective) training. Just ask your Shih Tzu! He'll tell you!

NOTE: Many dog lovers feel that the pronoun "it" is not appropriate when referring to a beloved pet. For this reason, Shih Tzu are described as "he" throughout this book, unless the topic specifically relates to female dogs. This by no means infers any preference, nor should it be taken as an indication that either sex is problematic.

1 *Why Train Your Shih Tzu?*

The Shih Tzu is truly an incredible dog. Few other breeds are as stunningly beautiful, impishly cute, and incorrigibly clever all at the same time. Ranked in the top ten most popular breeds by the American Kennel Club the Shih Tzu is small, doesn't shed (hairs remain in the coat until brushed out) and possesses just the right mix of sweetness and sass. As wonderful as the Shih Tzu is, however, he will need training.

Advantages to a Well-behaved Dog

Many pet owners, predominantly those who own breeds recognized for their good nature, often fail to invest much time or effort into working with their dogs. Generally speaking, these owners are under the misconception that a "good" dog doesn't need training. Unfortunately, this isn't quite right. A good dog is a trained dog. A congenial breed may be much easier to train than a more willful, dominant one but all dogs need training. There is no other way they can learn human rules.

For most pet owners, training a dog for the show ring or to compete in agility or obedience trials is not first and foremost

in their thoughts. (Once they discover how much fun it can be to train a Shih Tzu however, many change their minds.) The goals of training a puppy or dog tend to be much simpler. Usually, pet owners want to ensure that the dog understands a few basic commands, can be taken on walks without barking at other dogs or making crazy, zig-zag patterns underfoot, and knows and respects the house rules (no jumping on guests, eating from someone's plate at the dinner table, using the living room as a personal bathroom).

In the process of training a dog to adapt his behaviors to your human lifestyle, a few amazing things happen along the way. There are more benefits to a trained Shih Tzu than first meet the eye.

Benefit 1: A calmer household. A well-trained Shih Tzu has great house manners. He's up for fun whenever you are, but easily settled when you need him to be calm.

Benefit 2: Less destruction. A trained dog is usually not a bored dog. Training provides the owner interaction and mental stimulation that Shih Tzu crave. Training also requires a certain amount of physical activity—and the old adage, "a tired dog is a good dog," rings true.

A well-behaved Shi Tzu is a joy to be around.

Benefit 3: Easy leadership. How do you suppose owners of large, guardian breeds establish leadership in a non-confrontational way? They require their dogs to work for attention and food. And how do they do this? You already guessed it: they perform a series of training exercises every day. Asking your Shih Tzu to perform a behavior, getting a positive response from him, and rewarding that response generally go a long way to establish and keep a good leader/follower relationship between you and your dog.

Benefit 4: A more social dog. When you own a dog as adorable as the Shih Tzu, you want to be able to take him places and show him off. You can only do this if he's well-behaved and socialized. Training helps achieve these goals.

Benefit 5: A stronger bond. The more you work with your Shih Tzu and the more involved you are with him on a daily basis, the more amazed you will be with his mental and athletic potential and, more importantly, his capacity to love you.

Benefit 6: Improved senior years. Recent studies have shown not only that old dogs can learn new tricks, but that the process of learning helps maintain an older dog's cognitive abilities and helps to improve the quality of his life. With healthy Shih Tzu living well up into their teens, training at all ages can keep your dog feeling younger and live a more enriched life.

Simply put, enough good things can not be said about the benefits that training offers—not only for the owner but for the puppy, adolescent, adult, or senior Shih Tzu. You don't have to train beyond a handful of commands to reap a lifetime of benefits.

Bred for Companionship

The Shih Tzu is unique in that he is one of a handful of breeds not bred for a working purpose. The Shih Tzu was not bred to herd sheep, track rabbit trails, guard livestock, or be a watchdog. For centuries, the Shih Tzu's only purpose in life has been to serve as a companion dog.

Not have a "working" background has its plusses and minuses when it comes to training. Training your Shih Tzu will not be the same as training a Golden Retriever, but that's not a bad thing! Understanding the Shih Tzu's strengths and weaknesses when it comes to learning new skills will help you understand how best to approach training and get top results.

Here's a short rundown of some Shih Tzu qualities that can make training fun.

Harsh verbal corrections are never necessary with a Shih Tzu and may sour him on training completely.

Intelligence. There's no question that this breed ranks right up there with some of the canine world's best and brightest breeds on the doggie IQ chart. The breed is very adept at reading body language and almost intuitive in figuring out what's being asked of him. Intelligence is a great asset in dog training—if you can keep up with your dog!

Easily handled. Working with a small dog has many advantages, including the ability to easily transport your dog to various places to train. Little dogs can also be exercised more easily, making it less time consuming to "take the edge off" of a rambunctious dog prior to training sessions. Most owners tend to have more confidence in their own training abilities when working with smaller dogs, which

> **TZU TIP**
> **Little Dog Syndrome**
>
> *Owners of toy breeds often overlook behaviors that would be cause for alarm in a larger dog. Growling, snarling, and lunging at other dogs and people are commonly shrugged off as "acting like a big dog." No, this is just bad behavior! And, if allowed to continue, it can lead to more serious consequences—for the dog, owner, or both.*

Shih Tzu are smart, inquisitive, and love to be the center of attention.

including finding your dog to do spontaneous, quick, short training sessions. He's right there, so why not?

Playful and comical. What is it in the Shih Tzu's past that makes it such a crowd pleaser? This dog has a sense of humor and loves an audience. If you enjoy teaching your dogs parlor tricks (Shake, roll over, play dead), you are going to love working with your Shih Tzu.

Training Challenges

Of course, it's not all fun and games teaching the Shih Tzu. This breed's main purpose in life is to please and be pleased. Since Shih Tzu weren't bred to work with humans to accomplish a task, their approach toward learning new tasks is different than many of the breeds more commonly seen in obedience classes.

A few of the training challenges facing Shih Tzu owners include:

Boredom. The Shih Tzu does not do well working on the same exercise or skill over and over and over again. You can almost see their eyes glaze over and the enthusiasm fade. For this reason, training must be virtually indistinguishable from play for the Shih Tzu to excel.

Dubious work ethic. As noted previously, the Shih Tzu was not bred to work at anything. So, training sessions need to be kept in very short bursts, so that there's no "routine." His training sessions must always be changing, and kept interesting

translates directly into the dog having more confidence, too.

No inert drives. Without selective breeding to produce strong instincts such as guarding, hunting, tracking, scenting, retrieving, flushing, etc., the Shih Tzu has no intense genetic drives to distract him. That's not to say the Shih Tzu can't get distracted; it just means that this breed doesn't have generations of breeding to prewire him to respond in certain ways in certain situations.

Craves company. If you're in the kitchen, your pup will be underfoot. If you walk upstairs, don't be surprised to hear the quiet padding of your Shih Tzu right behind you. Taking a snooze on the couch? Your Shih Tzu will be right there, too. When a dog has a strong desire to be with his owner and/or family, this makes many aspects of training a bit simpler, and engaging. (If that description sounds a lot like "play," you're catching on!)

Intelligence. This works both for and against an owner, which is why this trait was also listed in the "positives" of training a Shih Tzu. Intelligent dogs learn quickly, but they can learn the wrong thing quickly. Shih Tzu owners need to be sure that what they teach their dogs is really what they think they are teaching their dogs. Shih Tzu retain knowledge well, so if he learns the wrong thing, it may take quite some time to undo the damage.

Size. Training a little dog requires a soft touch and a bit of dexterity and flexibility. You may find that working on some exercises with your Shih Tzu are backbreakers. The good news is that there are solutions to every problem and ways to save your back.

Easily distracted. The Shih Tzu can have a short attention span. In fact, some Shih Tzu appear to have no discernable attention span whatsoever. This issue usually can be solved by determining what is distracting the dog. For example, the dog may have better focus with treat training if he hasn't eaten recently or you train

right before a meal. A very lively, bouncy Shih Tzu may do better if he's just had a short play session or walk to burn off a little excess energy. And, every novice dog can focus better if there aren't any distractions such as other pets or people in the room.

Treat training fills 'em up. The Shih Tzu is little and as such, doesn't eat much on a daily basis. If you are using treats for training, it won't take too many before you lose his attention as his belly fills with food. Or, you could find that with all these extra treats, you are raising an obese Shih Tzu. (For ways to address this, see Chapter 7, "Home Schooling: Figuring in the Caloric Count of Treats.")

Shih Tzu love to learn new tricks.

The "plop" is one way a Shih Tzu will communicate that your training session is over.

Sensitive souls. This breed requires a light touch when training, both physically and verbally. He will not take impatient or gruff handling well; in fact, he'll take this roughness quite personally. Don't lose the fun and sparkle! Keep training light, enjoyable and most importantly exciting and the Shih Tzu will respond to your commands with joy—not because he feels he has to "or else."

Independent streak. Remember how the Shih Tzu wasn't bred to perform a working job? That means it is not inherent in the Shih Tzu to look to you for direction. As much as the Shih Tzu enjoys being around you, sometimes it will seem like he gets an idea and just sets off on his own. This can happen in the middle of a training session and is almost always accompanied by what Shih Tzu owners lovingly refer to as "selective hearing" ("If I don't make eye contact with mom then I really don't have to do what she's telling me to do."). To keep an independent streak from breaking up your training, you, as the owner, will need to be aware of your dog's willful moments and either finish training on a good note or make training so much fun that he doesn't have an opportunity to sour on training.

Clowning around. If you're taking training a wee bit too seriously or your dog is getting bored, the Shih Tzu may interject some antics of his own to lighten the mood. Take this as a sign that you need to lighten up your approach to training.

TZU TIP

To protect coat hairs when putting a buckle or clip collar on a dog with a full coat, part the hair just behind the ears and under the jaw. Then slip the collar into this part and fasten.

Harnesses are also very nice for training as they eliminate any stress on the dog's vertebrae. (They are particularly useful with small puppies who still haven't figured out that if they run 100 mph they will indeed hit the end of the leash and flip themselves.) Harnesses, of course, can be a little more difficult to put on a Shih Tzu with a full coat, but they aren't impossible. It's critical for both the dog and his coat that the harness fits properly and doesn't rub. If you have a small pet boutique in your area with someone who can give expert fitting advice, take advantage of this service and have her help you fit your Shih Tzu with a good quality harness.

detangler prior to a training session may help to prevent tangles from forming. You can work on artificial surfaces (indoors, outside on the sidewalk, in a training facility on rubber matting, etc.) but, you'll also need to do some work on grassy areas to give your Shih Tzu a full range of "distractions" for training—especially if you are interested in participating in obedience or agility competitions in the future.

After an outdoor training session, brush and maintain your Shih Tzu's coat as you would if you had taken him for a walk. If maintaining a full coat is hampering your desire to train, consider clipping your Shih Tzu. He'll still look adorable and his coat will be far easier to keep clean and tangle-free.

Another consideration with a full coat is the potential breakage of the coat hairs by a training collar. You can run damage

Smile, have patience, laugh at yourself, and strive to make training that much more enjoyable for both of you.

Coat Considerations

The Shih Tzu's beautiful coat raises some interesting, but not insurmountable, problems. First are the issues of matting and tangling from training in natural areas. Spraying your dog's coat with leave-in

Training in a full coat is not impossible.

Even a young pup can learn commands!

are much kinder on the dog's vertebrae than a thin collar.) Soft leathers, silky woven cottons, and smooth nylons may help to prevent hair breakage. Be sure to fit the collar so that two fingers can slide between the collar and the dog's neck.

Channeling the Positives

If you have purchased your Shih Tzu to be what it was bred to be—a constant, loving companion—you are going to thoroughly enjoy training your dog and will be able to experience the well-mannered fruits of your labor for many, many years to come.

If you purchased your Shih Tzu in hopes of producing an outstanding performance dog, you may want to lower your expectations a tad. There are incredible, high-drive Shih Tzu out there that win in agility trials and receive High in Trials in obedience. But these are more the exception to the breed rather than the rule.

What you can reasonably expect, with just a little bit of consistent, positive training, is a simply wonderful house pet. If you choose to continue on and train for obedience trials or agility competitions, a goal of earning titles in these sports is also well within the average pet owner's reach.

To have success at any level of training, it is most important to get to know the Shih Tzu, learn to love him for his strengths, and learn to deal positively with his challenges. Do this and you are almost assured of owning a charming, well-trained Shih Tzu.

control in this area by addressing the coat or addressing the collar.

To help prevent the hair shafts from breaking while the dog is wearing his training collar, make sure the coat is fully brushed before putting the collar on. When brushing the coat, spray it with a mixture of conditioner and water (or one of the many leave-in detangling conditioners) to keep the hairs hydrated, supple, and less likely to break.

Choosing a good collar can also help. The preferred collar for training a Shih Tzu is a flat buckle or clip collar—the wider the better. (Wider collars distribute the force of a tug against the leash more evenly and

2 What's Going on in That Brain?

When your Shih Tzu looks up at you with his big brown eyes, you can almost see his mind working in overdrive. Though small in size, the Shih Tzu is big on brains. Harnessing the "power of the pup" can be easy if you understand the basics of dog behavior.

How Dogs Learn

Entire books have been written on the subject of the cognitive abilities of dogs and how they process information. The subject is fascinating, but perhaps what is most interesting is that researchers may have found one of the reasons why the dog became man's best friend. Somewhere along the evolutionary line, dogs developed a higher understanding of and ability to interpret what we humans are trying to tell them.

Research shows that dogs will make eye contact with people to initiate communication and solve problems. Dogs also understand how to follow the direction of a person's point of the finger, a nod, a bow, or a turn of the head, something even rhesus monkeys cannot do without some training.

These findings may not sound like much, but it's actually very cool stuff, considering we've probably only scratched the surface in understanding the full extent of a dog's abilities. What's really important to take away from this research is that when it comes to living with people, heightened communication skills with humans have been critical to the domestic dog's success.

Visual Learning

So, you've probably lain awake at night wondering, "How do dogs learn?" Okay, probably not but, should you be curious, dogs are very much visual learners much in the same way as human infants.

If you are a parent or have worked with small children, you may already know that babies learn behaviors through mimicry. They watch and repeat the behavior if it makes sense to them. Recent studies have shown the same is true of dogs; however, the mimicry is not limited to a dog mimicking other dogs (i.e., interspecies). A puppy will mimic the behavior of humans as well as other dogs.

For example, if a dog is crated next to another dog and the other dog knows that pulling on a piece of ribbon releases a treat, the dog that is watching will be apt to try to pull the ribbon, too. The same is true if a dog is watching a person pull a ribbon; however, in the latter case, the dog must figure out how best to mimic this action on his own since he doesn't have hands. Seeing may not be believing, but it certainly is learning for the dog.

Body Language

Dogs depend largely on body language to communicate.

Ever wonder why Shih Tzu seem to recognize (and play really well with) other Shih Tzu? No one really quite understands it; however, it could be that within each breed's genetic code, there is something that allows members to more accurately" read" the subtle nuances of body language among fellow breed members.

TZU TIP

Physical differences between different breeds may throw the level of comprehension off at times (for example, a dog with prick ears may have a harder time understanding a dog with folded ears thinking that the upright ears are a sign of aggression. A dog with a docked tail may be confused by a dog with a full tail) but for the most part, unless a dog is socially inept, he can understand not only the basics of what another dog is communicating, but the nuances as well.

Hand Signals

Dogs are adept at watching and interpreting body language, which can be used to the trainer's advantage. Often it is easier to teach a dog a hand signal for a desired behavior than it is to attach a word to it. One reason is that when you give a command, such as *sit*, you may unintentionally say it in many ways.

"Sit," spoken in a soft voice could mean "Please sit."

"Sit" said with a little more authority could mean "Sit now."

Sit spoken with a bit of exasperation could be interpreted as, "I am so tired of you pacing the floor. You've got to sit before you drive me crazy."

"Sit" said in a cautionary tone might mean, "If you don't sit right now you are going to be in so much trouble."

And, "SIT!" when shouted could be taken to mean, "You are in big trouble!"

See how confused a dog can become with the multiple nuances of one simple word? And that's just one word from one person. If a dog lives in a house with other adults or children, imagine how many variations of *sit* the dog now must understand!

Contrast the variety of meanings of the spoken *sit* with a simple hand signal, such as a flat-handed, palms up motion. The hand signal is consistent; there's no difference in intonations. It is also consistent from person to person. A small child can give the same hand signal as an adult, as can a neighbor, and the dog recognizes the signal as the same from person to person.

Dogs learn hand signals as, or more, easily than voice commands.

Body language and signals are much easier for a dog to learn than words. With that said, however, dogs are also more adept at learning our vocabulary than was once thought.

Verbal Comprehension

At one time, it was a popular theory among some trainers that dogs didn't understand human language and that it was necessary to speak the language of "wolves." The theory had pet owners growling at their dogs, scruffing them on the necks, and throwing them into alpha rolls to show dominance. We're lucky more people didn't get bitten!

If humans are poor studies at understanding dog behaviors, we're probably even worse at trying to speak "dog." It doesn't work. We don't sound, look, or act like dogs.

Fortunately, dogs are capable of learning enough of our language that they figure out what we're saying pretty well. Some researchers estimate that a dog can learn at least 200 words and may be able to pick out more than one word from a sentence in order to make sense of what you're saying or asking him to do. So, asking a Shih Tzu to learn a handful of commands should not present a challenge to either dog or owner. What is important is keeping the commands or words consistent, and keeping the tone and intonation of the commands or words as constant as possible.

Key Periods

There are several key learning periods during a Shih Tzu's life. Understanding when these periods occur and what the implications are to the Shih Tzu's ability to learn are helpful to the owner in understanding how to approach training the puppy, young adult, and aging senior.

Neonatal. Puppies are born with their eyes closed. In addition, they aren't quite finished developing many of their sensory abilities. Despite this, research has shown that picking up puppies and stroking them gently for several minutes every day can make them more receptive to touch and more social toward humans later in life. Because this period is literally in the hands

Shih Tzu tend to recognize other Shih Tzu.

this point and can begin learning basic commands, Shih Tzu pups are still not very sturdy on their feet. Compared to other breeds, they are extremely slow in developing: they are slow to teethe, slow to develop immune systems, and slow to grow and thrive.

Six to Twelve weeks. Once the puppies are up and running (so to speak) and their eyes are fully opened, they begin learning how to get along with other dogs. They're prewired to understand how to communicate, but learning how to behave nicely with other dogs takes lots and lots of practice.

Your Shih Tzu will have learned the early rules of the road from his mom and littermates. Keep in mind that some dogs are better moms than others and the extent to which they teach their puppies not to bite too hard (bite inhibition) and to have good dog manners may vary.

What your puppy learns from his experiences with his mom, littermates, and other dogs in the breeder's home could vary dramatically depending on where he was raised. At a puppy farm for example, he

of the Shih Tzu breeder, it is important for the owner to know what kind of early socialization the breeder has given the puppy to better understand what issues the puppy may develop as he matures.

Two to Three weeks. Puppy eyes open about two weeks and hearing kicks in about a week later, so very early, basic socialization skills may begin when a puppy is three weeks old; however, until the Shih Tzu is more fully mobile (beginning at five weeks) the real socialization skills don't start.

Four to Five weeks. At this stage, the puppy's brain is getting closer to operating on full capacity. While larger breeds are capable of more complex learning at

A Shih Tzu's eyes do not open until two weeks of age.

may have been raised by an inexperienced or frightened dam, had little time with his littermates (since many are weaned very early for a quick sale), and had no interaction with other well-mannered, healthy, adult Shih Tzu.

Because Shih Tzu puppies are so slow to develop, they generally are not released to new homes until they are 12 weeks of age. Getting a Shih Tzu pup at 12 weeks (as opposed to eight) is good for a couple of reasons. Not only will the puppies have had lots of time to play with other dogs (both puppies and adults) but the knowledgeable breeder will have taken advantage of this time period to work on the pups' socialization skills with people.

If you purchased your Shih Tzu prior to 12 weeks of age, the responsibility for this critical socialization period and how it is managed falls on you. More on this later; however, it is important to know that it is not the quantity of experiences that

molds the dog during this time, but the quality of the experiences.

First Fear Period (Eight Weeks)

Right around week eight of a puppy's life, it appears that frightening experiences have a more traumatic and lasting effect on the puppy than perhaps any other time during his life. If your puppy is not sold until he is 12 weeks old and is with a knowledgeable breeder, this won't be an issue for you.

If, however, you are taking your puppy home at eight weeks, it is advisable to avoid things that could potentially scare your pup, such as not-too-friendly people or strange things or places during that first week. Or, if you do take your Shih Tzu puppy out and about, be careful to put your pup only in situations that you can control. Avoiding bad experiences at this point is more important than trying to rack up the positive experiences.

Also, whether your Shih Tzu is eight, 12, or 16 weeks old, it is important to understand that your puppy is not immune to disease. Until he has received his entire series of puppy vaccinations (usually between 16 and 20 weeks of age), your puppy can become infected with a deadly virus. (For more information on how to limit your pup's exposure to disease while he's receiving his vaccinations, see Chapter 4, "Safety First.")

Second Fear Period (One Year)

A second time period in which fearful experiences seem to have more permanent effects occurs roughly at about a

> ### TZU TIP
> Some research indicates that what you feed your growing puppy may affect his intelligence. Researchers for Iams released a study (2005) that shows the importance of at least two nutrients for the neurological development of a puppy's brain; in particular, the study noted that natural fish oils and "appropriate dietary concentrations of DHA [Docosahexaenoic Acid]" increase the trainability of a young puppy. As puppy foods begin to be offered on the market that are a direct result of this research, perhaps the real question is not whether you should feed your Shih Tzu "brain food," but rather if you're up to raising an even smarter Shih Tzu!

year of age. If you notice that your Shih Tzu is suddenly a bit more wary of things at this time, don't panic. It should pass, but just make sure that you watch for signs of stress.

Maturity (18 months to two years). When a Shih Tzu hits sexual maturity, a funny thing can happen: he may try to improve his pack status (if you have other dogs in the home) and/or exert his dominance with you or another household member. Fortunately, the Shih Tzu is not a breed that is inherently pushy. If you've been working on your dog's basic obedience, as well as good living skills, this period shouldn't present any problems.

Shih Tzu may be able to understand more than 200 words and short phrases.

Aging Shih Tzu. The Shih Tzu is a relatively healthy breed and many dogs can live fifteen years or more. Once your Shih Tzu hits ten or 12 years of age, he is considered a "senior." During this period of his life, it is important to continue to stimulate his brain and provide enriching activities for him. This, in combination with certain foods that are thought to help slow the degeneration of a senior

dog's cognitive abilities, can help your senior dog remain brighter and more aware well into old age.

During this phase of your Shih Tzu's life, it is important to keep providing new experiences—this can be accomplished with outdoor walks, visits to new locations, and training new commands, skills, or sports. Since learning may be a little slower, it's important to be patient, set your senior up for success in learning new skills, and keep it fun, as always.

TZU TIP

Researchers continue to delve into how nutrition can improve cognitive function in the aging dog. Foods enriched with antioxidants have been shown to reduce the behaviors related to cognitive degeneration and may possibly reverse some of the harmful effects of aging on a senior dog's brain.

Operant Conditioning

Understanding how dogs could be taught new behaviors and extinguish undesirable behaviors began in the late 1800s with Pavlov's famous experiment involving a

By the time a puppy is 12 weeks old, he has already learned much from his fellow littermates and his breeder.

group of dogs, a bell, and some food. In the experiment, the dogs would hear a bell ring and then were given food. Pavlov was able to condition a specific response from the dogs: when they heard the bell ring, they would salivate.

The experiment paved the way for future exploration into how dogs learn and from this, other researchers delved into the most effective ways to teach a dog specific behaviors. Modern-day training techniques have literally evolved from the laboratory into the field.

If you've done a little training in the past, you've probably heard the terms "operant conditioning" and "positive reinforcement." But, what do these terms really mean and how do they affect you and your Shih Tzu? Without going into tremendous detail and boring you beyond

tears (unless you're looking for a good way to fall asleep tonight), operant conditioning is the conditioning of an animal (be it a porpoise, dog, cat, bird, human, or wolf) to provide a specific behavior in response to a cue. In boiled-down dog-training terms, operant conditioning is training a dog to respond to a command or hand signal with the desired behavior.

Of course, there are many ways to get from point A (giving the dog a command) to point B (the dog gives the desired behavior). Positive reinforcement is a method of shaping a desired behavior, such as a *sit*, using something the dog sees as a benefit. In other words, if the dog does something correctly, he receives something pleasurable.

The opposite of positive reinforcement training is negative reinforcement training. As the name implies, this involves the dog receiving something undesirable in order to shape a behavior. This method works on the dog's desire to avoid discomfort or pain. An example of training using negative reinforcement to shape a behavior would be the use of a choke chain. A pop on the collar causes the dog momentary pain. The dog must figure out what he needs to do (or stop doing) to prevent the painful pop from happening again.

Reward-based Training

Though the avoidance of pain is certainly an effective way to teach a desired behavior, it is not any fun for the dog. Fortunately, in the past thirty years, advancements have been made in how to approach training. Trainers realized that rewarding a dog for providing the desired response worked just as well as punishing a dog for providing the wrong response. In fact, in addition to finding out that dogs learned quickly with reward-based training, it was discovered that the reward-based trained dogs retained the material well, without losing their enthusiasm.

Breaking it down. In order to make positive, reward-based training as effective as possible, there are a few rules to follow.

Rule #1: Set your dog up to succeed. The less chance your Shih Tzu has to fail, the more quickly he will learn the correct behavior. This is why, for example, when training a dog to sit, you will lure your dog into a sit, using a treat, before giving the command.

Rule #2: One will cost you 20. For every mistake you make in training your dog (i.e., you give your dog a command and he doesn't respond or gives the wrong behavior), it may take up to 20 correct repetitions to undo the one wrong action. If this isn't impetus for getting it right the first time, what is?

Rule #3: Take baby steps. When making an exercise more difficult, it's important to move very slowly and change only one variable of an exercise at a time. Variables can include: time (the length of time that the dog remains in a position); distance (how far away from the dog you move while the dog is in a position); or place (the setting in which you ask your dog to perform the behavior).

Rule #4: The eighty percent correct factor. Before increasing the difficulty of an exercise, it's important to make sure your Shih

Tzu has a solid understanding of it. If your pup is giving the correct behavior quickly and with confidence at least eight out of ten times, he's considered good to go. This does not mean you have to repeat the exercise ten times in a row. You will most likely lose your Shih Tzu's attention if you try to do this. Instead, break up the exercise throughout a training session or even throughout the day, asking for a few repetitions here and there.

Rule #5: Blame the trainer, not the dog. There are no stubborn Shih Tzu! If your Shih Tzu doesn't "do" a command or is having trouble learning a new skill, he is confused. Take a look at how you are approaching your training. Did you make too big of a step? Are you training too long and losing your dog's concentration? Are you making training fun? Usually, if you look hard enough you can find where there was a breakdown. Go back to making the exercise simpler and more enjoyable (and more playful) for your Shih Tzu and you should be able to roll right through your slight training bump.

Rule #6: Find what motivates your Shih Tzu best. Reward-based training involves rewards. For many Shih Tzu, treats work wonders but you might have a ball-crazy dog or one that likes to play tug. Take a little time to figure out what your puppy loves the most and use this for your reward.

Rule #7: Use treats as lures. With positive, reward-based training, you'll be using treats as a way to shape behaviors. For example, rather than pull up on your Shih Tzu's collar as you push down on his rear end to "force" a *sit*, you'll gently hold your Shih Tzu's collar as you pass a lure over his head to get him to fold into a *sit* on his own.

Rule #8: Fading is required. As your Shih Tzu learns an exercise, you will gradually phase out (fade) the treats used to shape the behavior. The next set of treats to fade will be those used to reward every correct behavior. You will always reward with praise and pats, but the treats will appear more randomly during training sessions.

Rule #9: Praise is the ultimate reward. Food rewards or playtime with a ball or toy are great rewards but your praise is what your Shih Tzu values most. Words of delight and physical pats and rubs are the ultimate reward for your dog.

Rule #10: It has to be fun. If your Shih Tzu doesn't think you're playing with him when you're training, then you're not making it enough fun for the dog.

Puppy Pointers

Puppies present a unique training problem to the owner: brief windows of opportunity. Very young puppies play hard, eat, relieve themselves, and sleep—not necessarily in that order. Finding a time when your puppy is focused enough on you to provide a productive training period can be difficult.

If you understand that your puppy can't focus for long periods (or take much of anything very seriously, for that matter), you've got a leg up on training. To be effective, you will need to keep your sessions exceptionally brief (maybe just a

> ### TZU TIP
> When using treats as lures and rewards, it's important that your Shih Tzu be a little hungry. If he's just eaten a meal, he won't be as motivated to work for food.

few repetitions of one or two exercises). Keep in mind that training can be impromptu and that you can perform these quick training sessions multiple times during the day.

When training your puppy keep these pointers in mind. In addition, here are some more puppy-training tips.

1. Always end a training session on a good note. Have your puppy finish with a successful repetition—it does not have to be the exercise you're working on, particularly if your Shih Tzu is having a difficult time.
2. Only train when you are in a good mood; your puppy will quickly sense your frustration, even if it's not with him.
3. Have lots of patience. Shih Tzu puppies are easily distracted by the tiniest of things. His attention span will improve as he ages. When you see that he is maintaining his focus a little longer, you can work up to longer training sessions.
4. Burn off a little steam. If your puppy has lots of excess energy and can't focus because he's really wound up, play with him. Play zoomie around the house. Toss a ball. Go for a little walk. Then get your Shih Tzu's attention for a mini training session.
5. Keep the puppy "joy" alive. Remember, it's easy to squelch your puppy's enthusiasm with just a single harsh word.

Working with Adult Dogs

Old(er) dogs *can* learn new tricks. In fact, the adult Shih Tzu will enjoy the extra attention she receives from you during training sessions. Training is also helpful in maintaining an elderly dog's cognitive abilities.

A benefit to working with the adult Shih Tzu is that he has a considerably longer attention span than a puppy. If you've adopted a Shih Tzu, you may find that your dog already knows a few commands.

A potential challenge to training an adopted dog is that it is possible that his previous owner may have been hard on him and possibly "soured" the dog to training. All is not lost if you suspect this is the case. If you make sure that training sessions do not remotely resemble work, your Shih Tzu will likely respond to them quite enthusiastically.

When working with a rescued Shih Tzu, be aware of potential "hot spots," areas on his body where the dog seems to be hypersensitive to touch. Painful experiences, such as being struck or grabbed roughly by the collar, will remain in a dog's memory for a very long time. If you find an area where your dog dislikes being touched, check with your veterinarian to make sure that your Shih Tzu is physically okay. If there is no underlying injury or disease that is causing pain, and you can pretty much narrow down the abnormal behavior as a response to touch or handling, then approach training keeping this in mind.

Older dogs benefit from the mental stimulation that training can provide.

The beauty of positive, reward-based training is that even the sensitive dog can be trained without being touched. As your adopted dog gains trust in you (and you in him) and his confidence levels rise, you will be able to handle him with fewer and fewer problems. He may never quite overcome his sensitivity to being touched in a certain area, but he will tolerate you touching him.

For most rehomed Shih Tzu, however, over-training or poor training aren't the issues; it's usually that the dog was turned over to a rescue or shelter because of a lack of training. Though working with an untrained adult dog can be challenging at first, once you've got the ball rolling and the adult dog begins to understand what this training thing is, she tends to learn very quickly.

Working on basic commands is extremely helpful in gently establishing who is the leader in your home. Training prevents a pushy Shih Tzu from becoming the self-appointed boss of the home. The more time you put in to your dog's training, the deeper your bond will be with your dog.

3 *Housetraining*

A major complaint among toy breed owners is that small breeds are difficult, if not impossible, to reliably housetrain. With few exceptions (usually due to health issues), nothing could be farther from the truth. Shih Tzu can be housetrained, and if given the right opportunities, can be trained quickly. Success in housetraining requires space control and scheduling—along with a little understanding about the differing needs and abilities of puppies and adults.

Understanding a Shih Tzu's "Sense of Space"

Puppies are born with an inherent desire not to soil their den. Shih Tzu puppies as young as five weeks old can be seen relieving themselves as far away as possible from mom and littermates when in the whelping box. Shih Tzu do not like being dirty or playing in urine-soaked papers. For even the tiniest of puppies, there is a well-defined sense of what area needs to be kept clean.

Housetraining, therefore, is simply taking the area that a Shih Tzu already feels is important to keep clean and gradually expanding it. The difficulty with training a toy breed is that the puppy's "sense of

personal space" is initially a very, very small area. A Shih Tzu puppy, for example, may be comfortable relieving himself at one end of a small crate if he can curl up and sleep at the other.

Space and Confinement

So, how small an area will your Shih Tzu keep clean? You won't know at first, so assume it's minimal. The best way to create an appropriate area for your Shih Tzu is to use a small dog crate. If the Shih Tzu physically takes up the entire crate with his body, there is no place he can go to get away from an accident. Therefore, in order to avoid urinating or defecating in his "area," he will hold as best he can and alert you to the fact that he needs to relieve himself.

Crate training only works if the crate fits and is used properly. When working with a crate, the basic rules for housetraining are as follows:

1. **Keep it small.** The crate should be just big enough for the Shih Tzu to stand up, turn around, and lie down comfortably. This means that a puppy will need two or three different crates as he grows. Another option is a crate that has a moving partition that can increase the size of the crate as needed.

Puppies are born with a desire to keep their den or nesting area clean.

2. **Make it comfy.** The crate should be lined with bedding that's warm, comfortable, and easily washed. Purchase two or three linings so that you can wash bedding as needed and always have another ready for use.

3. **Acclimate your puppy to his crate.** Crate training only works if your Shih Tzu is at ease in his crate. To help him get used to the idea that his crate is a comfort zone, keep the crate in a high traffic area, so he doesn't feel excluded. When he's out of his crate and you can supervise him, keep the crate door open, allowing him to go in and out at will. Other ways to help your Shih Tzu relax is to feed him and offer particularly yummy treats and/or safe chew bones when he's in his crate.

4. **Limit use.** Be careful not to overuse the crate. The maximum total amount of time a puppy or dog should be confined in a crate should not exceed ten hours (preferably only eight hours) in a 24-hour period. This does not mean it's okay to leave your Shih Tzu in a crate for ten hours straight without any breaks! And, this time total includes any hours during the night that you might keep him in his crate.

5. **Relief must be reasonable and regular.** It doesn't do any good to put a Shih Tzu in a crate, and then ask him to hold his urges beyond what he can reasonably maintain at his age. He will either dirty himself or put himself at a higher risk for constipation or a urinary tract infection by holding too long. To set

your dog up for success, make sure that his potty breaks are at regular intervals.

6. **Listen to your puppy.** Can you recognize your puppy's "I need to go" bark? When you hear it, don't ignore him. Take him outside to relieve himself and praise him. You want him to signal to you that he has to "go." And, you want him to recognize that you will take him out when he asks.

7. **Consider a "custom" training approach.** If you can't be home at regular intervals to relieve and walk your puppy during the day, then strict crate training isn't going to work. Don't panic! There are other ways to house-train dogs that can be very successful. (For alternatives, see Chapter 3, "Indoor Training.")

Timing Is Everything

Most housetraining "mistakes" occur when the dog is right under the owner's nose. Supervising your puppy or rescued adult dog while he is out of his crate is important for house-training success. Knowing when your pup will need to relieve himself helps, as does recognizing your Shih Tzu's telltale body language.

The "When." Puppies and adults need to relieve themselves immediately upon coming out of a crate and first thing in the morning. During waking hours, young puppies usually need to relieve themselves roughly every two hours. Raucous play sessions usually get the Shih Tzu's metabolism moving—another cause for a "bathroom" break. Then there's the time period of roughly 30 minutes after eating that gets the gastrointestinal system awake and active, and your pup or adult will need to relieve himself.

The "What." The body language of a dog that needs to relieve himself is pretty

Circling, sniffing, or retreating to a less populated area are all signs of a dog's need to relieve himself.

basic: he stops what he is doing, starts sniffing, and may circle. The only problem is that young puppies sometimes don't realize they have to "go" until the very last second. In these cases, the excited puppy may drop a toy, sniff once, squat, and "oops," there's a mistake.

The "How Long." If you are housetraining an adult Shih Tzu, he should have the physical ability to hold his urine and bowel movements for many hours at a time during the day and for at least eight hours during the night. A young puppy will be able to hold his bowel movements for several hours at a time, but getting control of urination can be a different story.

The general rule of thumb is that you can't expect your Shih Tzu puppy to hold for more than a couple hours at a time (during waking hours) until he is about four months old. Sometime between four months and five months of age, he will physically be able to hold up to four hours at a time during the day. (He will be able to hold longer at a younger age at night.)

TZU TIP

When you take your puppy or adult Shih Tzu outside to relieve himself, hang a ribbon from the door handle with a few bells knotted to the ribbon. Before you open the door, help your Shih Tzu bat the bells with his paws. He will learn quickly that if he rings the bells, the door opens and he can go outside to relieve himself. Soon, he will ring the bells to alert you that he needs to "go."

As the puppy continues to grow, the time period during which he can hold increases. By the time your pup is six to seven months old, he can control his bladder for up to six hours during the day; however, it is never advisable to make your Shih Tzu go more than six hours at a time without a potty break. If your work schedule doesn't allow this, it is best to come up with an alternate plan to allow your Shih Tzu to relieve himself on a regular, frequent schedule.

Regular feeding times help to make for a more predictable housetraining schedule.

Strive for Success

You can help ensure that your Shih Tzu holds to the best of his abilities by making sure of several things. First, he must relieve himself prior to being left alone. Second, your Shih Tzu must have had enough exercise and play to be calm and relaxed while you're gone. Third, your Shih Tzu needs to be comfortable in the space in which you've left him; if he becomes very upset or stressed when left alone, he most likely will need to urinate, defecate, or both, often within a half-hour of being left.

Finally, your Shih Tzu cannot be left in an area that is larger than his current idea of what his space is (i.e., the area that he wants to keep clean). For example, if your Shih Tzu is in the early stages of house-training, his "area" may be limited to his crate. An older puppy may have expanded his sense of area to a playpen, a young dog may be left safely in a room, and a seasoned adult dog may be allowed to roam freely through the home.

Food Matters

When trying to establish a routine and schedule for housetraining, it is helpful if your Shih Tzu eats his meals at regular intervals. Free feeding (keeping dry food available at all times) creates an erratic eating schedule, which in turn creates unpredictable needs to defecate. If possible, at least while housetraining, keep a regular feeding schedule and pick up any uneaten portions after 30 minutes.

Continue to feed your Shih Tzu the same food that he was receiving at the breeder's or shelter. Changing food suddenly can cause intestinal distress, which will complicate housetraining. If you must change

YOUNG PUPPY SCHEDULE

Time	Activity
6:00 A.M.	Relieve, feed, water, light exercise.
7:00 A.M.	Relieve again, confine*.
9:30 A.M.	Relieve, water, confine*.
12:00 P.M.	Relieve, feed, water, light exercise.
1:00 P.M.	Relieve again, confine*.
3:30 P.M.	Relieve, water, confine*.
6:00 P.M.	Relieve, feed, water, exercise.
6:30 P.M.	Play with puppy, watch for signs that he needs to go, and take out as needed; provide constant access to cool, clean water.
8:00 P.M.	Relieve, light exercise (be careful not to play with the puppy so hard that he needs to drink heavily. If he does drink heavily, take him out one more time just before you go to bed).
8:30 P.M.	Bedtime.
3:30 A.M.	Relieve. As the puppy gets older, sleeps more soundly, and is better able to hold his urges through the night, this break will shift to 4:00 A.M., then 5:00 A.M., etc., until he's going through the night without a break.

*Confinement describes a crate (for those who aren't home and can't supervise the puppy) or a puppy exercise pen (for those who are home and can provide close supervision).

foods, do so gradually over a five to ten day period, replacing more and more of the old food with the new food each day.

Developing a Schedule

When your pup or adult comes home, his needs will be a bit erratic. Everything is new and exciting, which can throw off his appetite, as well as cause increased stress and activity, which in turn will cause his water intake to increase.

Life will settle down after a day or two but in the meantime, you can use one of the two sample schedules (one for pups, one for adults) and tailor it to your Shih Tzu's individual needs.

If it is not possible to come home from work to relieve your Shih Tzu, consider hiring a dog walker or a trusted neighbor to take on the dog duties. If you have an older puppy (at least six months of age)

TZU TIP

Keep a log of your Shih Tzu's activities for the first week. It will allow you to identify any patterns that your puppy or dog is falling into and help you customize a more comfortable housetraining schedule for you and your Shih Tzu.

OLDER PUPPY OR ADOPTED ADULT SCHEDULE	
Time	*Activity*
6:00 A.M.	Relieve, feed, water, light exercise.
7:00 A.M.	Relieve again, confine.
12:00 P.M.	Relieve, feed, water, light exercise.
1:00 P.M.	Relieve again, confine.
6:00 P.M.	Relieve, feed, water, exercise.
6:30 P.M.	Playtime, watch for signs dog needs to go, take out as needed, unlimited water.
8:00 P.M.	Relieve, to bed.

or a playful, dog-friendly adopted adult, look into enrolling your Shih Tzu in a reputable doggie daycare.

Cleaning Up Mistakes

No matter how vigilant you are and no matter how well your Shih Tzu is progressing in his house-training, you will find a wet spot or a "gift" at some point in your dog's training.

When this happens it's very important to do thorough cleaning. Dogs have a tremendous sense of smell and if the job is not done properly, they will find their "spots." Finding a scent in the home is akin to receiving permission to relieve himself in the same spot again.

If the surface is hard and non-porous, you're in luck. You can remove the offending mistake and clean with most

Drinking after exercise means that an additional potty break will be required later.

household cleaners. Be aware, however, that products containing ammonia leave an odor that is quite similar to urine. The dog will realize that it's not his urine but the cleaner will leave a urine-like smell that may encourage your dog to use the same spot again.

A better cleaning solution to use when removing housetraining errors is a product designed specifically to break down uric acid into other compounds. The resulting compounds won't smell like urine—to the dog or you—and can be blotted up from the floor.

If the accident is on a carpeted surface, more aggressive cleaning is required, particularly with urine spots that have soaked through into the carpet padding. Blot up as much urine as possible before using a cleaner. When you use a cleaner, use a product that breaks down urine (as mentioned above) and follow the packaging instructions. Don't wait to clean it up later! If the urine soaks through the pad to the subflooring, your only real opportunity to rid the floor of urine odor is to replace the carpet and seal the subflooring.

Some trimming and additional cleaning may be needed with a full coat or a long clip to help keep furniture, rugs, and bedding free of fecal debris and urine.

Clean Coats

Keeping your Shih Tzu's coat clean, so that it does not transfer urine or fecal matter to other areas of the house, such as furniture and bedding, will help with housetraining. Once the smell of urine or waste becomes attached to a spot, the Shih Tzu may see this as an excuse to relieve himself in that area.

Males may need the hairs around their genitals trimmed to keep their bellies from becoming soaked with urine. Both male and female coats may require trimming and occasional washing around the anal area, as well, depending on how the coat parts and lies in this area. (Have an experienced breeder show you how to trim these areas or have a groomer perform these tasks.)

TZU TIP

If you are having new carpet installed, consider a pet-proof carpet padding. This product has been designed to allow for easier clean up of mistakes by preventing urine from soaking through the padding and into the subflooring. Also available is a brand of carpet with a waterproof barrier to prevent the carpet padding from becoming soiled.

Indoor Training

Many Shih Tzu puppies and adults live in apartments and condominiums that aren't conducive to frequent trips outdoors for potty breaks. If you and your Shih Tzu reside in a high-rise apartment or similar housing, take heart: it is entirely possible to housetrain your Shih Tzu in an area indoors.

Paper training. In the old days, apartment dwellers conquered this situation with newspapers. This method of training is still perfectly acceptable. Cover the floor of the room where the puppy is staying with a thick layer of newspaper. At first, it may seem like the puppy is going everywhere; however, within a matter of days you'll notice the puppy is choosing a certain place to eliminate. When this occurs, you can begin gradually removing newspapers in the areas that he keeps clean.

Gradually is the key here. With a very neat puppy or adult, you may be able to trim down to an area of one or two newspapers wide within a couple of weeks. A young puppy may take several weeks, or even months, longer.

Pee pads. Training with pee pads is exactly the same as training with newspapers—except that pee pads won't leak or soak through thanks to their absorbency and a waterproof backing. Many pee pads also have a slight odor that attracts the puppy to eliminate on them.

As the pup (or adult) gets the idea to eliminate on the pee pads, gradually remove the pads that aren't being used so that only one remains. This pad can be firmly anchored to the floor with a frame that is sold in stores to securely hold the pee pad in place. (More than one dog has found it fun to shred and play with the pee pad.)

Dog Litter boxes. Litter boxes aren't just for cats. Several are designed specifically for toy and small-breed dogs. You can also make your own litter box. The bottom half of a medium-sized plastic crate works very well for this purpose. Puppies and dogs don't like to step in their own excrement and, unlike cats, they don't bury their waste. The larger the litter box, usually the better the puppy or adult dog takes to it.

If your Shih Tzu is already trained to use pee pads or newspapers, you can begin by lining the litter box with them and place a few pads or newspapers around the box. If housetraining is completely new to your Shih Tzu, you can go ahead and fill the pan with roughly one inch of dog litter.

Your initial goal is for your Shih Tzu to enjoy being in the box. Make it fun for him to jump in and then out of the box. You can use treats to help lure him. Don't allow food bits to fall into the box itself;

TZU TIP

Dog litter is usually made of pelletized, recycled newspaper. Using kitty litter is not advised since these sandy types of litter will get caught in your Shih Tzu's pads and coat (especially if he's not clipped) and will track through your home. Additionally, the sandy type litters can be dusty and could be inhaled by your Shih Tzu.

dogs have a natural aversion to soiling areas in which they sleep or eat.

Leave a little scent in the box for your Shih Tzu. A small scrap of paper with your dog's urine on it or a tiny piece of fecal material should be more than sufficient.

Then, as often as you can—and particularly at those times when you know your Shih Tzu needs to relieve himself (immediately upon waking in the morning or after a long nap)—put him in the box. When he eliminates in the box, praise him.

When you can't watch your puppy, set it up so that the puppy sleeps in a small area (such as his crate) and then steps out of his den immediately into the litter pan. As your puppy figures out the routine, you can expand his personal space to a small exercise pen, placing the Shih Tzu's bed or a comfy crate in the pen with the litter box.

Eventually, you should be able to give your Shih Tzu access to a large exercise pen or small room with a litter pan while you are gone. If at any time there are mistakes, decrease the Shih Tzu's free space, making it easier for the dog to succeed.

When working with a litter box, keep in mind that it will have an odor. So, when considering where to keep the litter box, weigh this with where your Shih Tzu is comfortable relieving himself before deciding on a permanent location.

Balcony Options. If your apartment or condo has a balcony, it is possible to train your Shih Tzu to use the "facilities" outdoors.

When using an outdoor litter box on the balcony, make sure the space itself is safe for your Shih Tzu. Puppies can easily squeeze through most balcony bars, so it

will be necessary to put up additional fencing. Also, some Shih Tzu are good climbers and jumpers, so make sure the fencing extends beyond the possibility of a dog's wildest leap, which is as high as five feet. Consider roofing the area in which your Shih Tzu has access on the balcony to ensure there is no chance that he can fall.

Accident or Symptom?

Most housetraining problems can be chalked up to the dog being allowed too much freedom too quickly or to accidents that weren't cleaned up sufficiently.

There are occasions, however, when the accidents can be caused by an underlying health or behavioral problem. Some diseases and conditions that can cause accidents include urinary tract infections, canine cognitive dysfunction, diabetes, incontinence, certain medications (such as Prednisone), separation anxiety, phobias (thunderstorms, fireworks, etc.), and territorial marking.

If your Shih Tzu previously was doing well with his housetraining, or if you own an adult Shih Tzu that suddenly begins having accidents in the home, take him to the veterinarian for a check-up. Keep a log of when the accidents seem to be occurring along with the dog's feeding and exercise schedule and any other changes you might have observed to help your veterinarian solve the puzzle. Often, accidents that have a biological or behavioral factor can be eased through medications, training/behavior interventions, or a combination of both.

Home Schooling

will recognize the *go potty* command and begin to look for a place to go.

Timing

A large portion of housetraining success relies on your timing—both with praise and corrections.

Praise

Praise your Shih Tzu every time he relieves himself in the proper place, be it outdoors, on a pee pad, or a litter box. Don't get too excited or go overboard in your verbal enthusiasm; he may stop what he's doing and get excited too, which would slow the connection between relieving himself and being a good boy!

If your Shih Tzu loves treats, you can give a food reward every time he relieves himself appropriately. Phase out the treats once he starts getting the idea; otherwise, you risk creating a treat monster that begs to go outside and "try" every few minutes in order to get more treats.

"Go Potty" Command

A command that is very helpful when traveling with your Shih Tzu or when you are asking your puppy or dog to relieve himself at a strange location is *go potty*.

To get your Shih Tzu to associate *go potty*, or any other words you choose to use, with the act of relieving himself is simple. Say the words several times while the puppy is urinating or defecating and then say, "good boy!" Over time, your Shih Tzu

Corrections

The only acceptable time to correct a Shih Tzu for urinating or defecating in the home is if you can catch him in the act. The correction must only be verbal. A simple, "Ah-ah!" and/or a hand clap will be enough to stop most puppies in midstream.

Keep in mind that when your Shih Tzu makes a mistake, no matter how frustrated you are or how much you paid for that exquisite Persian rug, you must not lose your temper. There's no need for strong corrections in housetraining. Most accidents are the owner's fault anyway, with the most common errors either giving the Shih Tzu too much freedom in the house too soon (remember that much smaller sense of personal space with a little dog?) or simply not paying attention and catching the body language of a dog that needs to go.

"He was getting back at me for..."
Many owners swear that their dogs are relieving themselves inappropriately in the home, "because he's mad at me." They take the act of defecation or urination by their dogs personally.

There is nothing personal about a dog relieving himself in the home and a dog will not relieve himself out of spite. The dog's reasons are much simpler. Usually he had the urge to go and was given too much freedom, too soon. Alternately the dog could be suffering from separation anxiety or one of several health conditions (see **"Accident or Symptom?,"** page 29).

If your once reliably trained Shih Tzu suddenly becomes unreliable, don't blame it on the dog's ill mood; check with your veterinarian to rule out a health problem.

Marking

Training male Shih Tzu not to hike their legs indoors can be difficult. If you keep your eye on your young male puppy as he begins to become sexually mature (around six to seven months when he transitions from squatting to hiking his leg), you can prevent him from getting in the habit of marking your chair legs, cabinets, and cupboards by keeping a close eye on him.

If you catch him hiking his leg to mark, say, "Ah-ah!" or a sharp, "No!" Some trainers recommend purchasing a washable "belly band" to prevent territorial young males from hitting their marks in the home. A belly band is a six-to-seven-inch-wide cloth with an absorbent pad that wraps under the dog's belly and fastens with velcro over (or on) top of his back, acting like a male diaper, of sorts. When he tries to urinate, he urinates in the pad. This solves the

To keep your yard in top shape, give your Shih Tzu the "potty" command where you want him to relieve himself.

problem of items in your home receiving a shot of urine, but it doesn't necessarily stop the behavior. The Shih Tzu may be discouraged with a wet band and stop hiking his leg *or* he might continue to hike his leg, not seeming to care if he urinates in the belly band.

Whether you use a band or not, prevent marking in its early stages by watching your dog carefully and verbally correcting him if he's caught in the act. If you can't be home at all times to watch a young male—or if you've adopted a male Shih Tzu and don't know if he wants to mark or not—confine him to a crate when you're gone.

Intact males are much more likely to mark then neutered males. If your male Shih Tzu is not a show prospect, consider neutering him to prevent several undesirable male behaviors.

TZU TIP

A Shih Tzu-sized dog door can be set in virtually any type of door. The easy-swinging flaps allow the dog to go in and out at will. If you choose to set up a dog door, be careful about the puppy or adult's outdoor access. You might consider only allowing the Shih Tzu to exit the dog door and enter an outdoor pen with an overhead covering to protect from the elements and predatory birds.

4 *Socialization*

Today we have higher expectations than ever before for our pet dogs, requiring them to be friendly and sociable, not only with immediate family members, but a whole host of other folks. Fortunately, the Shih Tzu is by and large a naturally friendly, outgoing breed, so nurturing a puppy to be a friendly adult is typically a skill that most every Shih Tzu owner can achieve.

A Social Breed Needs Socialization?

For more than 150 years, the Shih Tzu has been bred exclusively for human companionship. So, why does a social breed need "socializing?"

The reasons are twofold. First, not every Shih Tzu puppy is born with a terrific temperament. As the popularity of the breed has mushroomed, more and more people have gotten involved in producing Shih Tzu pups with less and less concern for temperament (or health or conformation). As a result, timidity and fearfulness have become increasingly common in the "less well bred" puppy. Puppy buyers cannot assume that just because a puppy is a Shih Tzu, he will have a fantastic temperament.

Second, socialization is a skill that requires constant practice throughout the life of a dog. The naturally, super-friendly puppy (that has had great human experiences) can regress in his socialization abilities if he's not given the continued opportunity to meet pleasant people as he grows and matures.

So, whether your Shih Tzu began life as a disadvantaged puppy or was born into the best of all worlds, a social adult dog is the result of regular, positive exposures to nice people. The more positive meet-and-greets the puppy has, the more he will grow to realize that people are good and can be trusted. With this approach, fearful dogs will become less timid or wary and gregarious puppies will continue to be social butterflies.

Socialization Begins at Home

It is critical for your Shih Tzu to be comfortable with everyone in your household. Children, older parents, and significant others should all spend time getting acquainted with the puppy and forming a loving, trusting bond.

It's also important to make sure that your puppy is comfortable with anyone who comes into your home on a regular, semi-regular, or even sporadic basis. This includes friends, your children's friends, neighbors, grandparents and/or grandchildren. Don't forget those folks who may be in your home when you are not, such as the babysitter, a petsitter, cleaning person, or a health aide who provides assistance to an older family member.

You'll also want to make sure your Shih Tzu puppy is comfortable with people he may come in contact with outside the home. For instance, if you visit with a relative who lives in a retirement or assisted-living community, make sure you take along your puppy so he can become comfortable with the different scents and abilities of older people, such as braces, canes, crutches, walkers, and wheelchairs, etc.).

Conversely, if you live in a retirement community and will have grandchildren visiting you (or if your neighbors frequently entertain their grandchildren), you will want to make sure your Shih Tzu is comfortable with young children. An adult dog (of any breed) that has not been exposed to children often can be uncomfortable or fearful of a young child's loud outbursts and erratic movements.

Quantity vs. Quality

You may have heard that you should try to introduce your puppy to 100 new people in the first month he is home with you. That breaks down to roughly three or four new people every day.

Making tons of introductions to people is terrific if all of these introductions go smoothly, if all the people are friendly and aren't intimidating, and if your puppy is eager to meet new people. Unfortunately,

By nature, Shih Tzu are friendly, outgoing dogs that love people.

this is rarely the case. Every puppy has his comfort zone. Some puppies can be easily overwhelmed and are more reactive to loud sounds, erratic movements, or uneven gaits. There are going to be times when your Shih Tzu puppy is going to be uncomfortable. A meeting that causes the puppy stress is not a quality experience.

Additionally, there are going to be limits as to how many people, places, and things you can physically introduce your puppy to on a daily, weekly, and monthly basis. That's okay. Do not beat yourself up (or allow others to chastise you), if you can't introduce your puppy to a few new

Ask children to sit when introducing them to your Shih Tzu.

people each day. A few new people each week is fine.

The key to developing a social Shih Tzu is to make sure that the experiences your puppy does have with people are positive. In other words, while quantity is nice, the quality of the people exposures is what is critical. Keep things upbeat and comfortable for your puppy and you will help your Shih Tzu to develop into a people-loving adult dog!

Safety First

When you first bring your puppy home, he will be approximately 12 weeks old.

Until he has received his second or third (or even fourth) round of vaccinations, your veterinarian may not feel comfortable recommending that you take him to public places. How at-risk your puppy is to deadly viruses varies with the presence of outbreaks in your community. Your veterinarian will be the best possible guide as to when it's safe to allow your Shih Tzu puppy's paws to touch surfaces in common areas, so follow his or her advice.

If you are not able to take your puppy out for several weeks, you can still work on socialization within your home. In fact, some veterinary behaviorists advise spending the first week allowing the puppy to bond to family members and become comfortable in the house before opening your door to all those folks who are eager to meet your new puppy.

The reason for this wait is sound: a puppy will be much more confident meeting strangers if he already trusts his human family. And, your puppy will look to you for direction. If you have a solid trust established your pup will turn to you when he confronts something that he isn't quite sure about.

Your veterinarian will be able to tell you when it's safe to take your puppy to public areas.

If you have a self-assured manner and exude confidence, your puppy will pick up on this and in turn will be more confident in his approach to something that may have made him a bit wary just moments before.

Off-leash, In-home Socialization Tactics

The beauty of having your puppy meet and greet new people in your home is twofold. The puppy will be comfortable in what he considers his territory and he will be able to meet all these new people off-leash.

When a puppy is off-leash, he can make his own approach to a stranger. Since no one is holding or restraining him, he will come up to the new person at a pace that is comfortable for him. For some Shih Tzu, this will be a flying, whirling mass of silky hair, syncopated steps, and lots of licking. Others will be a little more cautious—and that's fine, too.

When inviting people into your home to meet your Shih Tzu, help the greeting go smoothly.

1. Avoid meetings at the front door.
2. Ask your guest to pick up a few treats at the door or just inside the door.
3. Require that your guests remove their shoes before walking into your home. (This limits the potential for tracking diseases into the home before a puppy is completely immunized.)

4. Instruct your guest to completely ignore the puppy when entering.
5. Have your guest sit down quietly and talk conversationally with you, still ignoring the puppy.
6. Allow the puppy to take a few small treats from the person's hand.
7. Patting should be on the side of the puppy, not the head.
8. Have a basket of favorite toys so the guest can interact with the puppy.

Meeting People Safely

Until your puppy has been cleared by your veterinarian to set paw in areas that might put him in contact with viruses, you will need to be creative in providing safe

One safe place to meet new people is right in your own backyard.

Veterinarian's office: Your veterinarian and his or her staff will know exactly how to approach your puppy and help socialize her. Unfortunately, the veterinarian's office is much like the pediatrician's—filled with sick patients. So, take precautions and don't allow your puppy to set foot on the floor, or sniff things in or outside of the office.

Outdoor cafés: Purchase a nice screened stroller for your puppy and secure him with a harness and clip to prevent him from leaping out. Park your stroller and puppy at a local bistro or café and enjoy a cool or hot drink while people stop to ooh and ahh. Give passers by a little treat to offer your puppy.

The Coast Is Clear

Once your veterinarian feels comfortable allowing your puppy to go out into the world to meet people, you can do just that! Keep in mind that now you will be meeting and greeting people while your Shih Tzu is on-leash.

opportunities for your puppy to meet friendly people. The following are a few places that can be safe for young puppies if the proper precautions are taken:

Pet stores: Your puppy can meet-and-greet people at the local pet shop if you don't allow him to touch paws to the floor and if you ask people to cleanse their hands prior to petting. (Carry wipes with you; most pet owners don't mind a quick wipe of the hands if you ask them.) Put your puppy in a dog stroller (one that you've purchased and know is sanitary) or use the store's shopping cart (wipe it down first and place a clean towel or blanket in the cart.) Be sure to attach a safety harness to the cart to make sure your pup can't jump out.

> ### TZU TIP
> *Some training classes are offered for young puppies with as few as one round of puppy vaccinations. Though some experts recommend these classes to puppy owners, others do not as these classes are not totally risk free. Before taking your Shih Tzu to an early puppy class, consult with your veterinarian and thoroughly discuss the risks involved and the quality of the training program.*

The Rules for On-leash Meet and Greets

1. **Allow the puppy to make his own approach.** This is perhaps the most important principle of all, and one that often very well-intentioned dog owners don't follow. In most cases, your Shih Tzu will be straining at the leash to say "hello" and will be a mass of wriggling, bouncing puppy. That's what you want. Allow him to go up to the person (if the person has asked to pat him), and allow the puppy to meet the stranger.

   If, however, your puppy appears to be hesitant, don't pull him over to the person, push him forward, or pick him up and hold him for the person to pet. Instead, permit him to back up to where he is comfortable and watch from there. If your puppy is displaying a mix of signals (wriggling to see the person, but also showing signs of being a bit timid), give him a second to sort everything out. When the signs of fear are gone, allow him to make his own approach.

2. **Pick your people.** Not all people are nice. Not all people are friendly. Not all people like dogs—not even cute, fluffy puppies. Sometimes our dogs figure this out before we do. When socializing

A veterinarian's office can be a great place for your puppy to socialize with experienced dog people.

   your puppy, introduce him to people who are friendly, quiet, and want to meet him. With a puppy as cute as a Shih Tzu, it's pretty easy to determine who is a likely meet-and-greet candidate and who is not.

3. **Set the rules.** When your puppy goes up to meet people, you don't want him getting frightened because they get too squeally or can't resist putting their faces in your puppy's face. Hugs, bending or reaching over the dog to

TZU TIP

Many people think that most dog bites arise from confrontations with aggressive animals. Actually the opposite is true: fear is the number one cause for dog bites.

pat him, grabbing at the puppy, or attempting to pick him up are all potentially frightening gestures to even a confident dog.

So there will be times when you'll need to run a little interference for your puppy. If you're not comfortable telling strangers exactly how you want them to greet your puppy, be selective. Choose people with whom you are comfortable or seek out people who already know how to approach puppies: veterinarians and their staffs, dog trainers, dog owners who are members of dog training clubs, breeders or members of conformation clubs who exhibit their dogs, and members of Shih Tzu play groups, to name just a few.

4. **Avoid a crowd.** Children in particular like to converge on puppies. Can you

blame them? (No one wants to miss out on a puppy snuggle!) As excited as children can get when they see a puppy, you need to gently ask them to be quiet and have them take turns saying, "Hello" to the pup. When confronted with several young children, ask them to line up "short to tall" (this exercise usually quiets them down as they figure out who's grown the most). Then one at a time, allow each child to sit down and let the puppy crawl into his or her lap.

5. **Use treats.** A common training practice is to give little treats to strangers to offer your puppy. This works on several different levels. If a pup learns at an early age that an outstretched hand means a treat, he will be highly unlikely to snap at it—treat or no treat! Additionally, on a more basic level, the Shih Tzu associates good things with people. That's really the goal of this exercise. It also allows the puppy to make the approach to the person, not vice versa.

6. **Keep it positive.** Though a cautious puppy requires a little extra awareness on the part of the owner when making introductions, it's often the overly exuberant puppy that presents puppy owners with a quandary. The problem here is that the really outgoing, enthusiastic (and excitable) puppy may get so wound up meeting new people that he starts jumping up, lunging at faces to give kisses, hopping on his back legs and scratching at the person to be picked up, or even urinating in his

An example of happy body language: note that even when lying down, this Shih Tzu's tail is up!

The slight drop in this Shih Tzu's tail is a transition sign.

excitement. What you don't want to do with this happy puppy is squash his enthusiasm for people by harshly disciplining your puppy when he's making his greeting.

If you say, "No!" to your puppy or yank on the leash to gain a bit more control, you've effectively told him he's not supposed to be happy about meeting people. A better approach—one that will help to keep your pup's love of people intact—is to work on the pup's obedience skills (a nice *sit* would work fine) and try to be a calming influence. For example, you can kneel down and gently restrain the pup so he can't jump up to lick someone's face or inadvertently scratch the person's legs while trying to get picked up. You can also warn people that your puppy gets a little excited and then kneel down to gently restrain him. Most people won't mind an excited puppy, but you will need to work on his manners so that when he's older, he won't jump up on people. Eventually he'll learn that if he keeps his paws on the ground, he will get all the pats he can stand!

7. **Watch your puppy.** To keep all greetings pleasant, watch your puppy and try to understand what he is telling you. If he's happy, the meeting is going well. If he shows signs of being unsure, give him time to size the situation up and put a little more space between the stranger and him.

Give friendly strangers a treat to offer a less confident adult dog.

months rarely will show aggression, no matter how frightened they might be. Adults and puppies over the age of five months are more apt to react to fear.

When working with an adult Shih Tzu with limited socialization (or a rescued Shih Tzu that may be uncomfortable with certain people), go slowly. If he's happy and relaxed, have people offer treats and pats only if all is going well with no signs of stress. If the dog appears stressed or is giving some mixed signals (he's furiously wagging his tail but his ears are flattened), back him up and give him a little more space. Ask the stranger to toss him a treat instead of hand feeding it.

If you don't know what to expect from your new adult dog (maybe you've adopted him from a facility that doesn't do any temperament testing) or you are having a hard time "reading" your dog, go to a dog-training facility. Here you'll find lots of dog-savvy people and experienced dog trainers or behaviorists who can help you.

Socializing the Adult Dog

The good news about socialization is that the more effort you put into making your Shih Tzu more social and accepting of all types of people—at any age—the more social and accepting she will become.

With an adult dog, particularly one that is a little wary of strangers, it is exceptionally important to watch body language. Never allow the adult dog to become stressed. Puppies under the age of five

Fear Factors

Not all Shih Tzu are born to be the life of the party. If you find yourself with a fearful puppy, don't dwell on it. No puppy or dog is perfect—and that's okay! As soon as you realize this and accept this, you can really enjoy your puppy and help him to be all that he can be.

Do you love your Shih Tzu? Does he love you? That's what's important. If you've got a shy or wary Shih Tzu, work

Timid puppies require a more watchful owner who is adept at reading his or her puppy's body language in order to make sure all socialization experiences are positive.

on it! Allow your timid Shih Tzu to make greetings on his own terms (off-leash in the home or another safe environment), with no one trying to reach down to pat him, pick him up, or even make eye contact.

Be patient. Certain groups of people may always intimidate your Shih Tzu. If you know what stresses your puppy or dog, that's half the battle. You can work on the rest. Just don't push and always, always, always remember that if you aren't comfortable working with your dog yourself, seek professional help. For a listing of professional organizations, see "Behavior Training," under Useful Addresses and Literature, page 141.

Allow a shy puppy to meet and greet new people on his terms.

Home Schooling

Reading Your Dog's Body Language

Fortunately, the Shih Tzu is fairly expressive in his body language and is considered one of the more easily "read" breeds of dogs. A happy Shih Tzu is generally pretty easy to spot: a wriggly, loose body; soft eyes; wagging tail and an overall appearance of joyfulness. If you've had your puppy for a week or more, you're probably pretty good at recognizing when he is truly happy, comfortable, and good with the world.

When socializing your Shih Tzu with other dogs, you should be able to recognize a change in his behavior. If you can recognize the moment your Shih Tzu's demeanor changes, you can prevent a bad experience for your dog. Be aware of the moment that flag-like tail goes slightly still, the second he stops his four-paw dance, and take notice before your Shih Tzu becomes afraid or takes an aggressive stance.

The moment you see your Shih Tzu transition from happy body language, stop the approaching person and give your Shih Tzu a moment to size up the situation. If you can't stop the stranger from coming closer to your Shih Tzu, move your dog to a comfortable distance and let him observe from there.

Resist picking up your dog (unless he is in an absolute panic) or trying to comfort him with your voice. At this moment in your puppy's life, you need to be the embodiment of self-confidence. Once your puppy returns to being his happy self, you can continue on your walk.

If your puppy never stops showing friendly, confident behavior, allow him to meet the person you are approaching. Remember, it's all about making sure your Shih Tzu is comfortable when he's meeting people, so that he learns that people are not something to be feared.

Basic Body Language

The following are some basic body "speak" that you will easily recognize with your Shih Tzu. Remember, the most important body language to recognize is the absence of friendly behaviors. Stressed, fearful, or aggressive behaviors can be avoided if you recognize the transition moment.

Happy Body Language

Tail, tail, tail. The Shih Tzu's tail arcs over the body and really wags when the puppy is comfortable and happy.

Soft eyes. A relaxed dog has a certain gentleness to the eye.

Loose body. You know how your puppy's body swings when he walks and appears completely relaxed? That's a good sign. A loose-bodied dog is a dog comfortable with where he is and who he is with.

Smiling. Some dogs show their teeth in what really looks like a smile. Frequently mistaken for a snarl, this "smile" is not accompanied by any sounds, but is seen with happy dog body language. The smile is considered to be a submissive behavior by some behaviorists; others feel it is a dog's attempt to mimic a human's smile. Either way, it's all good if accompanied by tail wagging and a loose body.

Relaxed ears. The contented Shih Tzu's ears will either be in a normal, folded resting position or held in a calm, but interested, forward position.

Open, friendly mouth. The happy pant is seen with a relaxed body and a tired puppy, giving the Shih Tzu the appearance of an open-mouthed smile.

Unless a Shih Tzu is tired, a yawn is a sign of stress.

Stressed Body Language

Droopy or overly stiff tail. If that arced tail drops and goes limp, your Shih Tzu is experiencing some form of stress. If the tail becomes stiffly arced and almost rigid-looking at the base, he is moving into an aggressive posture. If the tail tucks between the legs, he's very afraid of something or someone.

Half-moon eye. A half-moon eye is seen when a Shih Tzu shifts his eyes to look at something without moving his head. This sideways glance creates a white, moon-like sliver on the side of the eyes. When the whites of a dog's eyes show in this way, something is of concern to him.

Panting. The nervous pant is accompanied by a more taut, anxious appearing body and a tightening around the eyes.

Closed mouth. If a panting Shih Tzu suddenly shuts his mouth, this could precede a bark, snap, or lunge.

Flattened ears. Shih Tzu have very expressive faces and much can be told from the positioning of their ears. When a dog's ears flatten against his neck, he is very uncomfortable.

Lip licking. Nervous lip licking makes it appear that the dog is repeatedly trying to lick the tip of his nose or the air in front of his mouth.

Yawning. Unless your puppy is genuinely tired and curled up on his bed, yawning at other times is usually indicative of a dog that is feeling increasingly uncomfortable.

Extremely Stressed Body Language

Shaking, cringing, frantic pawing at your legs, hiding, crying, whimpering, tail tucked, ears flattened. All are signs of extreme fear; the Shih Tzu may also urinate submissively.

Intense staring, stiff-bodied, hackles up, rigid tail wag, standing on toes, growling, snarling, snapping, lunging. All are signs of aggression, which is often a result of fear. If your dog feels he can't retreat or run away, he will begin posturing and if this doesn't work, growling, snapping, and lunging to create more space.

5 Developing a Dog-friendly Shih Tzu

In a perfect world, every Shih Tzu would get along with every dog he meets. In the real world, however, just being a dog doesn't guarantee instant membership in the "I Love All Dogs" club. Regardless of where your Shih Tzu stands on the social scale, providing the right kind of experiences can improve your Shih Tzu's comfort level around other dogs.

Every Encounter Counts

Just as positive meet-and-greets are important in developing a human-friendly Shih Tzu, positive introductions and opportunities for polite, friendly play are equally essential in developing a dog-social dog.

And, as you probably guessed, it's not so much how many dogs your Shih Tzu puppy meets but how well these meetings go. One bad experience with another dog can leave a lifelong impression. Likewise, a few excellent experiences with really nice, kind dogs can help your dog become more confident with other dogs.

If your Shih Tzu is timid around other dogs or just not very tolerant, continued efforts to socialize him will improve his

comfort level with other dogs. If on the other hand, your Shih Tzu is already the happy guy on the block, continued, positive interactions with other friendly, polite puppies and dogs will help you keep your Shih Tzu dog-friendly.

The Puppy Learning Curve

All dogs are born knowing how to communicate—at some level—with other dogs. This basic ability is literally in a dog's DNA.

Years of breeding for certain qualities, both physical and mental, have influenced each breed's ability to communicate both within the breed and with other breeds and mixes. Some dog breeds are very expressive and their intentions are easily interpreted by other dogs. Think of these dogs as the "type O positive," or the universally understood canine.

Then there are breeds that are less expressive, more subtle in their body language, or even known for giving muddled or mixed signals. These dogs get along well with dogs that communicate in the same way as they do but may easily confuse (and offend) other dogs.

Shi Tzu are social dogs that enjoy having good play buddies.

Finally, there are breeds (and mixes thereof) that are genetically predisposed to be a bit confrontational with other dogs. Terriers are famous for their "pluck," which is sometimes described as a willingness to stir up a little trouble given the right set of circumstances.

Where does the Shih Tzu fall in all of this? As you probably guessed, the Shih Tzu tends to be quite social by nature. They're not easily offended by other dogs' behaviors and are quite patient when it comes to trying to figure out what another dog is trying to communicate. Shih Tzu are known for being non-confrontational and if faced with a bully, will most likely say, "I give!" rather than try to stand up to the offending dog.

With that said, there are definitely Shih Tzu out there that don't fit the breed mold. Some will gladly confront other dogs just to let them know who's boss. There are also Shih Tzu that are so timid or fearful of other dogs (even those that are half their size) that they aren't comfortable being around them. Where did these behaviors come from?

Genetics certainly plays a role in the Shih Tzu's temperament and how an individual dog interacts with other dogs, but, the dog's life experiences, beginning at birth, play an enormous role in how social a dog will be as an adult.

In other words, you can't control what your Shih Tzu has naturally inherited but you can give a puppy (or an adult) the help he needs to behave nicely around other dogs.

Early Advantages

Puppies need to practice good greeting behaviors, friendly play positions, and appropriate (and inappropriate) touching and sniffing.

If a puppy is removed from his litter-mates and mom too soon and/or has no contact with other dogs for months, the little guy can become so awkward with his attempts to communicate with other dogs that by the time he is a young adult, his communication skills are so off that other canines have difficulties understanding his intentions—or worse yet, take offense at the young adult's attempts to greet or play.

An enormous advantage to purchasing a puppy from a knowledgeable breeder is that the puppies will remain with their littermates until they are 12 weeks old. These puppies have a tremendous base in good dog behaviors.

Bite inhibition is perhaps the biggest of these lessons—helpful not only for dog-dog relations but for the humans living in the house with the new puppy. The puppy learns from play biting his littermates (and being bitten by them) just how hard is too hard.

The puppy also learns how to play nicely. The gung-ho puppy realizes that no one likes it when he plays too hard or too long. In fact, his littermates won't play with him if he's rude. The puppies practice their greetings, invitations to play, posturing, and submissive gestures, learning that good behavior begets good things. Poor behavior means no one plays with you and if you aren't careful and you're really naughty, mom will let you have it.

Many Shih Tzu puppies are sold at younger ages. Does this mean he'll turn into Dogzilla, trying to put the fear of Shih Tzu into every dog he meets? Will his lack of dog experience make him

"Dad" can be a terrific role model for teaching puppies good dog behavior.

eternally terrified of all things walking on four paws? Absolutely not!

It just means that with less "puppy experience," your Shih Tzu may be a little less skillful in understanding other dogs and being understood himself. With practice, he can get better!

Safe Socialization

Before widening your pup's social circles ask your veterinarian about the risks of contracting canine viruses. In areas of recent outbreaks, your veterinarian may caution against any interactions until the pup has finished his complete series of vaccinations. If the risk is slight, puppy socialization may be approved (with restrictions) after just two or three sets.

Places to Avoid

Whether the risk is small or very real, the following dogs and dog areas are considered high risk and absolutely off-limits to all puppies until they are completely vaccinated.

- **Veterinarian's office:** Attend appointments as needed but keep clear of other dogs. Many of the animals at the vet are there because they are sick. Don't allow nose licks, sniffing the floor, paws on the floor, or contact with any animal or surface that an animal has touched other than the examining table (which presumably has been thoroughly sanitized between patients).
- **Dog parks/runs:** Going to a dog park with a young puppy is a huge health risk and a non-negotiable no-no.

Safer Options

■ **Your backyard:** If you don't already have healthy, vaccinated adult dogs in your home to play with your newest addition, you can invite friends to come over with friendly, healthy, fully vaccinated adult dogs.

■ **Shih Tzu play groups:** The sponsors of these groups tend to be experienced, knowledgeable Shih Tzu breeders or fanciers who demand the same level of safety for their own dogs as you do for your new puppy. Most groups require proof of vaccination and will require that the puppy has had his second or third round of puppy vaccinations.

■ **Homes of friends and neighbors:** If you have a neighbor with a patient, adult dog or a fully vaccinated puppy, and you feel comfortable that his or her yard hasn't been contaminated by any sick dogs, you can allow your puppy to socialize there.

A healthy, vaccinated adult dog can be a good choice for a young puppy to meet in your backyard.

Best Playmates

The Shih Tzu, though sturdy for his size, is not a big dog. To be safe, choose puppy play partners that are roughly the same size as your Shih Tzu. Adult dogs should be no more than double the size of your Shih Tzu in weight. A friend may have the gentlest, most loveable Lab on the block, but the size difference between a five-pound Shih Tzu puppy and a 75-pound adult Retriever is just too much. One clumsy move on the Lab's part and your Shih Tzu could be injured.

Though dogs are required to be healthy and fully vaccinated to play in these areas, this is not well-regulated and can be the source of many deadly outbreaks. Wait until he's completely vaccinated and proceed with caution (see "Homeschooling: Dog Park Basics, page 54).

■ **Public parks:** If there are high numbers of dogs, on-leash or off, there's a higher chance that someone has a deadly virus or is shedding a virus.

■ **High dog traffic areas:** Any pathway or grassy areas frequented by neighborhood dogs on a regular basis puts your pup at risk.

These two adult Shih Tzu have similar play styles—and get along well—with the young Havanese on the left.

Seek out puppies and dogs that have similar play styles to that of a Shih Tzu. The Maltese, Bichon Frise, Havanese, Miniature Poodle, Cavalier King Charles Spaniel, and Pomeranian are just a few of the non-sporting and toy breeds that have similar manner of play.

Don't equate small size with compatible play style. Many terriers are of similar size to the Shih Tzu, but their love of all-out, body-slamming, break-neck play behaviors and tendency toward high arousal can intimidate or frighten a Shih Tzu.

You should also steer clear of breeds bred to hunt down and kill small animals.

> ### TZU TIP
> Don't introduce dogs to each other in one or the other's perceived territory. Dogs are naturally protective of areas they think of as "theirs." Choose a neutral setting instead.

The hopping and pouncing your Shih Tzu does when playing can quickly trigger prey drive.

Making Introductions

There are several ways to introduce your puppy or adult Shih Tzu to another dog. Side-by-side walking in a neutral area is one of the least confrontational. Have the owner of the other dog you want your Shih Tzu to meet walk with you for about 10, 15, or even 20 minutes. Keep the dogs far enough apart that they can't make any contact with each other. Your goal is for them to eventually walk quietly and in a relaxed manner. Often this is all it takes for the dogs and/or puppies to learn enough about each other to be comfortable playing (or ignoring each other) in an off-leash area.

Mouth licking is a submissive and friendly gesture.

To introduce the dogs off-leash, use a dog gate, fence, or similar barrier between the dogs in a neutral spot. This way the dogs can see, smell, and watch each other in the safety of their own area. A timid dog knows he can retreat at any time, and neither dog's movements are restricted.

Watch the body language of both dogs. Do not allow the dogs to physically meet until both are displaying very friendly behaviors. If a dog is becoming too excited or shows some signs of stress toward the other dog, remove the dog from the barrier and allow him to watch from farther away. When he's relaxed you can try again.

Staring, growling, barking, or a stiffening of a dog's posture are all signs that the offending dog(s) need to be moved farther apart.

Controlled play can occur when both animals are giving off good signals. Allow the two dogs to play off-leash in an enclosed, neutral area. Start with short bursts of play, calling out your Shih Tzu to keep things from getting too rough. As you get a feel for how the dogs get along, you can allow them to play for more extended time periods.

The perfect play buddies are those that understand and respect each other's play and can settle themselves down for breaks. If the dogs or pups aren't taking breaks, you will need to call them out to give them a few minutes of "quiet" time.

TZU TIP

Though owning a social dog is fun, if your Shih Tzu is not comfortable around other dogs, it's not the end of the world. It's more important that your Shih Tzu be friendly to people.

Dogs that play well together will naturally take breaks.

Handling On-leash Aggression

Dogs tend to "grow" a bit when on-leash, particularly the smaller breeds. You may notice that your Shih Tzu barks and lunges at other dogs when he's on-leash, but is completely docile when he's off-leash. That is usually because he thinks you'll back him up when he's on-leash or because he's a bit fearful and feels he can't escape—the best defense is a good offense.

Regardless of the reasons, on-leash aggression can develop into a bad habit very quickly. And, because of his small size, the Shih Tzu that incites another dog is likely to wind up the injured party.

Though some people find it cute to see a little dog act "big," it's important to realize that the leash-aggressive dog is misbehaving! If you find your Shih Tzu behaving irritably toward other dogs while you are walking him use these tactics.

- When you see even the slightest attitude change, calmly move your dog farther away from the other dog.
- Distract your dog by doing a quick succession of obedience exercises. Reward him for being good and keep moving away from the other dog.
- Keep the leash loose. A taut leash relays increased stress to your dog.
- Don't use a retractable leash. A four- to six-foot leash provides much better control.

Remember your dog is no less of a wonderful companion, even if he exhibits a bit of leash aggression. Work to help him become more comfortable walking near other dogs. With practice, he will get better.

Introducing a Second Shih Tzu

"Hard-to-have-just-one" is a common syndrome among Shih Tzu owners. After having raised one Shih Tzu, you may feel the need to add a second to your life. The good news is that this breed tends to get along very well with others. It's possible not only to add a puppy to a Shih Tzu family but also a rescued adult dog.

Whether you are adding a puppy or an adult dog to your Shih Tzu family, the basic principles are the same: watch for signs of stress and take it slow.

When sociable, friendly canines are introduced correctly, the introduction and acceptance process usually moves along quickly. (Shih Tzu are famous for making instant friendships with other Shih Tzu.) However, don't think all is lost if it's taking more than a couple of weeks for your resident dog (particularly if he is not a Shih Tzu himself) to accept a new companion. Sometimes it just takes a little while.

How to Proceed

First impressions do count when it comes to welcoming a new Shih Tzu into the family. Whether you're bringing home a puppy or an adult, it's important to keep the drama between the dogs to a minimum—or non-existent, if possible.

Stage 1: Begin with separation. Remember that your home is currently your resident dog's "territory." When you bring in a new Shih Tzu, your resident dog may question why he's there. Realizing that the new Shih Tzu is a family member

> ## TZU TIP
> Make sure your reasons for adding a second Shih Tzu are good ones. Add to your canine family because you want another dog, not because you believe your Shih Tzu would like a companion. Most Shih Tzu are perfectly content to be an only dog.

takes time for some dogs. In order to allow the Shih Tzu to make non-confrontational introductions, keep the dogs separated but within view of each other. Place the new Shih Tzu in an exercise pen or a crate, or use a dog gate to separate the dogs. Allow the dogs to sniff and interact on either side of gate, making sure that all interactions are positive.

The moment one of the dogs begins to appear stressed or shows signs of aggression or fear, move the aggressor away from the gate. You don't want to see any hard stares, stalking, barking, or growling. Once the dogs have settled down, allow them to see each other through the barrier again. Praise good behavior; treat the resident dog for happy body language. Be patient and don't give up—it can take time! When the dogs seem to be ignoring each other, move to Stage 2.

> ## TZU TIP
> If you have more than one resident dog, choose the most congenial—and lowest on the totem pole in ranking—to introduce to the new dog. This allows the new dog to have a buddy. You can work up from there, one dog at a time.

Stage 2: Start side-by-side walking. This exercise takes two people and a little energy. Try to walk the dogs (the new Shih Tzu and the resident dog) for 15 to 20 minutes twice a day. (If you have a new puppy, this time will be much shorter as the pup won't have much endurance.) Don't allow the dogs to sniff each other or play together on-leash; walking will give them the opportunity to learn more about each other without the stress of physical interaction. Your goal is for the dogs to ignore one another or start showing friendly body language. If they start bouncing around playfully, that's even better!

Stage 3: Add small amounts of time to play together. Once the dogs show no signs of aggression or fear (this could take a single walk or a few days) allow the dogs to play with each other for a very limited time—as short as two to five minutes initially. Don't overreact to the dogs' interactions with each other, but watch for signs of stress and separate as needed.

Stage 4: Spend more time together. If short play periods are going well and if the dogs ignore each other when separated, show friendly behaviors, or exhibit a desire to play, you can allow the dogs more play time together. As always, watch carefully to make sure neither dog is taking offense to anything the other is doing. Adult dogs tend to be more tolerant of puppies, but this is not always the case. Be respectful of an older dog's desire to be left alone.

Stage 5: Final melding. If extended periods of play are going well, you can increase the amount of time the dogs are together as long as you are there to supervise. Keep in mind that even if it appears all is going

> **TZU TIP**
>
> To help the resident dog associate the presence of the new Shih Tzu with good things, be sure to give the older dog more of the things he thinks are really special: attention and love from you, walks, treats, good bones, and more feedings (break up allotted food into smaller servings) can help soothe jealousy.

well, dogs will be dogs and arguments can erupt over things as slight as an accidental bump, the discovery of a long lost toy, or a disagreement over who gets to lie where on the dog beds. These squabbles usually won't happen if you are supervising (and are in a leadership position) but they can occur if the dogs are home alone. It's always wise to crate or separate the new puppy or dog from the resident dog for several months or longer when they are left alone.

Even when the new Shih Tzu appears to have bonded with the resident dog, it's advisable in the first few weeks to keep them separated when you aren't home.

Home Schooling

Dog Park Basics

Dog parks are becoming increasingly popular and are popping up in cities and suburbs all over the country. Well-run dog parks give opportunities for both dogs and their owners to socialize, but they can also be the site of some serious dog injuries.

Guidelines for Safe Fun

Follow size segregation. Look for dog parks that separate dogs by size. Most limit the small-dog area to 20 pounds and under. Never, never, never (no matter how hard he pleads) allow your Shih Tzu to play with medium or large dogs. If the dog park does not segregate by size, it is not a suitable play area for your dog. Period. Even with a 20-pound limit, make sure that the dogs in the area are appropriate. Some of the smaller terrier breeds fitting this weight classification have very high prey drives and can turn a fun game of chase into a more aggressive sport.

Make introductions slowly. The best way to introduce your Shih Tzu to the other dogs in the dog park is to use the staging or holding pen. This is a small area, usually no more than six or eight feet wide and long. Once you're in this area, let your Shih Tzu sniff the other dogs through the fence. There's usually a lot of excitement at first; this is not the time to let your Shih Tzu join the pack. Wait until the other dogs lose interest in your dog and go back

to playing farther away in the yard. Once they aren't crowding the entrance, you can let your Shih Tzu enter.

Stay off-leash. Though it may seem scary to let your Shih Tzu run with strange dogs without restraint, it's actually safer. Without a leash, he will be able to make the correct greeting behaviors. Additionally, if he has a tendency to be leash-aggressive, being off the lead makes this a non-issue.

Call your dog out frequently. If your Shih Tzu shows any signs of stress or if you think the play may be getting too rowdy, call your dog out of the play group. Give him a ten-second break before allowing him back to play. This gives everyone a little time to settle down. Good play buddies do this naturally; dogs that are getting to know each may take a little while to initiate breaks during play.

Consider a harness. If you're not sure your Shih Tzu will come to you when called, purchase a comfortably fitting harness that has a small handle or grip so that you can lift him out. Remember that whenever you reach in to separate dogs, there's always the risk of getting bitten. It's always better to call your dog out of a potential fray, if possible.

Leave if necessary. Expect to see some unsocialized dogs and uneducated owners, often together. Dogs may be behaving like bullies (chasing other dogs, or pinning them aggressively), while the owners simply stand by as if nothing is wrong. To avoid confrontations between dogs (or owners), remove your dog from the dog park.

Keep it moving. Dogs tend to get in trouble when they play in one spot for an

Shih Tzu tend to get along well with other Shih Tzu; introducing a new dog generally isn't a problem.

extended period of time, especially if their owners are not watching them for signs that the play is going awry. To keep things fun for your Shih Tzu, continually walk through the park. This will keep your dog moving and will help to create the natural breaks needed during high-speed, wild play.

Be flexible. Even a friendly, gentle, well-socialized Shih Tzu won't like every dog he meets. If there's a group of dogs that your Shih Tzu finds offensive or he simply is not interested in playing, try another time. The dogs and owners you find at the park in the afternoon could be totally different than those who bring their dogs in the evening.

Avoid high-usage times. Some dog parks are just too popular. There may be too many dogs in too small an area. If you find this to be the case in your local dog park, try visiting at other, less populated times.

Follow the rules. Every dog park has its rules posted and most require that all dogs be current on their vaccinations and have proof of vaccination and/or a dog license. Females cannot play at the park while in season; intact males usually are not allowed if they are 12 months or older.

Have fun! Dog parks are often just as much about human socialization as they are about canine fun. It's a great place to meet friendly owners who like their dogs just as much as you do. Just don't get so involved in a conversation that you lose sight of your Shih Tzu.

6 *Habituation: In and Out of the Home*

Some Shih Tzu dogs appear to be absolutely bomb-proof. Whether it's a thunderstorm, low-flying fighter jet, a dropped pan, or kids on scooters, nothing fazes these dogs. Part of what makes these dogs so calm is their inherited temperament; however, usually behind every well-adjusted Shih Tzu is an owner who has spent time helping the dog feel comfortable with a variety of different noises, objects, and places. Habituation is the key to a happy, secure Shih Tzu.

How Puppies Learn "It's Okay"

Canines are masters of detecting something "different" in the environment. Though some dogs have been selectively bred to be über sensitive to smell, sounds, and/or movement, all dogs possess these heightened senses to some degree, including the Shih Tzu.

Dogs have a highly developed sense of smell. Some have been reported to scent odor particles as miniscule as 500 parts per trillion. A dog's hearing is equally impressive, and can detect sounds at much lower volumes and wider frequencies than humans. Additionally, dogs can fine tune what they are listening to by pricking and moving their ears to get a better angle on the sound.

What we know about a dog's vision is evolving, and it appears there may be two types—a more central vision (like people's) and a band-type vision that possesses incredible peripheral sight. We do know that dogs seem to be better at seeing in dim light and detecting motion.

A Shih Tzu puppy has all these incredible senses. From an early age, he is hearing, seeing, and smelling much more than we can detect. All this "noise" would be enough to drive a human crazy.

The puppy, however, learns to cope with all this input with the help of her mother. Mom is the ultimate filter and training tool in teaching a young and impressionable puppy what requires attention, what can be ignored, and what is dangerous.

Reaction and Action

If a noise or object takes a puppy by surprise, he may startle. Depending on what he saw or heard, this is a completely

The mom serves as a filter for unusual sounds in the home, and the puppies take her lead in how they react.

normal reaction. What the puppy does next, the action he takes, is more telling about how well acclimated he is to the household.

Young puppies, when still with their mom, may initially jump at a loud noise or "scary" object, but will look back toward mom to gauge her take on the situation, instinctively following her lead. If the mom is a fearful, skittish, or overly wary Shih Tzu, her puppies will learn to have the same worries, too. Assuming he has a solid, well-adjusted mom, the puppy will usually investigate the source of the sound or ignore it.

For example, let's say a door slams shut in the home. The puppy is surprised by the sound and jumps a little. He looks toward mom, who doesn't react to the sound at all. She's heard it for years and it's no big

deal. The puppy may now be curious and go investigate the door or he may simply go about his business. If the puppy hears a door slam in the future, he is less likely to be startled and will likely adopt his mother's attitude toward the event.

Early Environments

Mom can only teach her puppies how to filter out sounds, smells, and potentially scary things if there are sounds, smells, and potentially scary things to filter. A dog raised in a kennel, though he may be clean, healthy, and possess a bright temperament, may not have experienced the sights and sounds of living in a home.

Puppies and dogs whelped and raised in the home have a distinct advantage over those Shih Tzu that were raised in more isolated environments because the home-raised puppies are exposed to all kinds of noises. They learn not to be afraid of the vacuum cleaner, music, television, people talking, loud laughter, the oven timer, a loud garbage disposal, alarm clocks, the doorbell, or loud knocks at the door.

If mom is well-adjusted to the home, then the breeder really doesn't have to do much work to help habituate the puppies, except to keep the pups in the center of the household and expose them to all the sounds and sights of everyday living.

Once you bring your new puppy or adult Shih Tzu home, be aware that there will be sights and sounds your Shih Tzu may never have experienced before. If you live in an apartment building, for

> ### TZU TIP
> It's difficult to produce bold, confident puppies from a timid or easily spooked mom. This is another reason why breeders should place temperament as a top consideration, right up there with health and conformation.

example, slick floors, buzzers, intercoms, staircases, elevators, and revolving doors may all be new experiences for your Shih Tzu. If you live in the suburbs, your indoor sights and sounds may be similar to the breeder's, but the outdoor environment may introduce completely different experiences, such as noisy school buses, rolling garbage cans, and delivery trucks.

Even if your puppy or adult dog is comfortable with his new home and his surroundings, it's a good idea to habituate your Shih Tzu to areas, homes, and businesses that you plan to visit—even if infrequently—with your dog.

Working with Reactions

As your Shih Tzu explores your home, yard, and neighborhood, he will encounter things she hasn't seen or heard before. From time to time these things will frighten or startle him.

If your Shih Tzu sees, hears, smells or otherwise detects something that worries him, there are several things that you can do to help him adjust.

As your Shih Tzu explores his new home, he may startle at objects he's never seen before.

1. **Be confident.** Remember, now that your Shih Tzu is no longer with his mom, he is using you as his filter. He trusts you and will look to you for your reaction. In other words, if you act like it's no big deal when the toilet flushes, he'll learn that the sound is no big deal. Your body language should exude confidence.

2. **Sit by the object or sound source.** Take a book or an article you've wanted to read and sit by the source of your Shih Tzu's concern. Let him see that it's no big deal—but don't try to cajole him over. Let him make his own approach. If he doesn't come over to investigate after a few minutes, that's fine, too. Try again another time.

3. **Praise good behaviors.** If your Shih Tzu goes up to the object or source of the sound (assuming it is not something dangerous), you can praise your dog. Your voice should be solid and pleasant, "Good job, Buster!" You can also toss treats near the object. If the toilet flushing is frightening to the dog, for example, he will find rewards (the treats) for approaching the toilet.

4. **Give him time.** Confident dogs generally adjust to new sights and sounds in the home more quickly than timid dogs. Be patient!

5. **Maintain a comfortable distance.** If you think something might rattle your Shih Tzu—or it would be reasonable for something to frighten him—allow him to see or hear the "thing" from a safe and comfortable distance. For example, on garbage day, allow your Shih Tzu to see the truck and all its movement and noises from the security of your home. If he's comfortable with this, watch the truck go by from your front stoop the following week, then from the lawn the next—and that's as close as he needs to get. For a school bus, work up to being on the street corner with the kids when the bus arrives.

Your body language is important to your Shih Tzu. If you exude confidence and a "no worries" attitude, he will pick this up from you. Reward good behaviors and ignore timid and fearful responses. Above all, allow your Shih Tzu to make his approaches according to his comfort level, not yours.

Don't Baby Your Dog

What do we want to do when we see a precious puppy jump back in alarm or a rescued adult dog cower in fear? We want to pick them up, cuddle them, and tell them everything will be okay. "Coddling" a dog, or trying to reassure a frightened dog with our voices and our touch, is a natural reaction for people. It is what we would do with our own children.

Dogs, however, don't interpret our actions as being reassuring. They read our actions as verification that they did the right thing: the object was scary and the

---

TZU TIP

Why do dogs love to bark, lunge, and bite at the vacuum cleaner? The machine may be emitting a high-frequency sound that is irritating or frightening to your Shih Tzu.

Shih Tzu was very wise to react in the way he did. Translated: you just praised your dog for being frightened. The next time he hears or sees whatever it was that startled him the first time, he will react in the same way.

It is far better to leave your Shih Tzu's paws on the floor and allow him to work out the situation on his own. The one exception to this is if your Shih Tzu frantically paws at your leg to be picked up. This is not the "I want to be petted," but "I am terrified. Please help me!" If your Shih Tzu reacts to a stimulus in this way, pick him up and remove him from the situation. You can set him back down when he is a comfortable distance away.

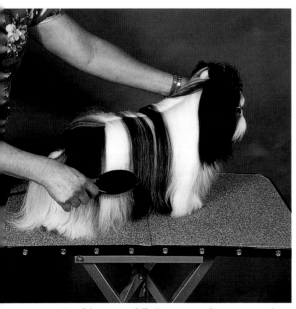

Teaching your Shih Tzu to stand on a grooming table will help with grooming chores, whether you plan to keep him in a full coat or clipped.

Acclimating to the Grooming Table

Habituation includes training your dog to sit, stand, or lie down calmly for everyday grooming and hygienic tasks. For those Shih Tzu owners who would like to maintain a full or longer coat on their dogs, this is particularly important.

One of the most important things you can train your dog to do is stand or lie quietly on a grooming table. A solid grooming table is a wise investment as it allows you to be able to work on your Shih Tzu without straining your back or trying to get him to lie still in your lap.

The grooming table is roughly three feet high, so few Shih Tzu will attempt to jump down. The table top should provide enough room for an adult Shih Tzu to stand and lie down comfortably and be surfaced with rubber to provide the dog with solid footing.

Carefully lift your Shih Tzu up on the table. Though most Shih Tzu are pretty bold and adjust to the table quickly, the first time up, most puppies and dogs may be a little nervous. To help a reticent Shih Tzu acclimate to the table, steady him gently with your hands. Praise him and if he'll take a treat, give him a food reward.

If your Shih Tzu is worried about the table, limit the time up on the table according to the anxiety level of your Shih Tzu. If he's trembling, keep him steady for ten to 20 seconds. If he begins to relax, you can keep him on a little longer. If he continues to tremble, gently ease him off the table. Try to work up to a few minutes at a time and give him lots of atten-

While working to acclimate your Shih Tzu to the grooming table, you should continue brushing him daily whenever you can.

tion. Never leave your Shih Tzu unattended while on the table. Keep at least one hand on him to steady him.

While you should praise and treat your Shih Tzu for good behaviors, be careful not to accidentally reward fearful behaviors by trying to verbally or physically reassure him. Keep the time periods short and try to end on a good note. Remove him from the table before he becomes impatient or restless. The goal is to get him to associate being on the table with good things.

Introducing the Grooming Loop/Noose

If your Shih Tzu acclimates to the grooming table and stays relaxed, you may not need a noose. This contraption is an L-shaped arm that attaches to the side of the table. An adjustable, padded collar hangs from a short length of line attached to the part of the arm. If you want to work on your Shih Tzu with both hands—or your puppy or dog is comfortable on the table but is very wriggly—the grooming noose can come in handy.

As with learning any new skill, go slowly when introducing the noose to your Shih Tzu. If he's comfortable with the table, attach the metal arm and noose to it, lift your Shih Tzu up and allow him to investigate. Praise and treat him for being curious.

Next, gently put the noose over his head, keeping the length of cord loose so

that your Shih Tzu doesn't feel any restraint. Praise and treat him for being such a wonderful dog. Each time you put your Shih Tzu up on the table and use the noose, you can shorten the cord a little more until there is just enough tension

TZU TIP

Never leave your Shih Tzu on the table in the noose unless you are right there by his side. It is very easy for a dog to misstep and fall off the table with his rear legs, causing a potentially deadly disaster. The noose is there to help steady your dog on the table and is not meant as a restraint to use when you need to answer the phone or check on something in the next room.

Begin grooming early so that when your Shih Tzu is an adult, he will lie quietly for even top-knot combing.

that he is comfortable standing on the table, but isn't tempted to move around or jump off.

Once you've reached this point, you can go back to brushing and grooming your Shih Tzu for short time periods in the noose. As he becomes more used to the noose and table system, you can increase the time in the noose until your Shih Tzu is happy to remain on the table for 30 minutes or however long it takes you to brush him out, clean his ears, brush his teeth.

Storms, Fireworks, and Other Scary Stuff

It is not uncommon for dogs of any breed to have a slight fear of thunderstorms, fireworks, gun shots, or other loud noises. Your Shih Tzu may initially startle at thun-

der, firecrackers, or a gun shot, but he'll usually figure out that he is safe and these noises won't hurt him. That's often true if you remain calm, you don't have any other dogs in the home that are terrified of the particular sound or event, and your Shih Tzu has a relatively calm demeanor.

There are some dogs, however, that truly are terrified by storms, fireworks, and gun shots. If this is the case for your Shih Tzu, there are a few things you can do to help him overcome these fears.

Exposure. You can play a realistic tape recording of the sound your Shih Tzu is afraid of (be it thunder, firecrackers, or gunshot) to condition him to the sound. Your dog will get used to hearing the sound and realize that nothing bad happens when it occurs. Playing a recording of the sound allows you to provide your Shih Tzu with more controlled exposures.

To use this method, play the recording quietly at first. Reward your Shih Tzu if he remains calm. If he shows signs of stress, ignore his behavior and reduce the level of the recording. Reward him as soon as he shows signs of being calm. Work up to longer sessions at increased volumes, until you reach a lifelike sound.

Though this method works with some dogs, often the sound that is frightening the dog has another element attached to it. In other words, it's not just the sound that terrifies the dog. With a storm, it could be the change of pressure. In this case, the dog may be totally okay with a

A fear of thunderstorms may be lessened with a combination of desensitization techniques and positive reinforcement.

recording of thunder, but will still be terrified of an actual storm.

Calming sounds and scents. Some research indicates that certain types of music played at low levels can be relaxing for dogs. CDs of music designed just for canines are available and are worth a try with your Shih Tzu. Holistic veterinarians feel that using a few drops of Rescue Remedy (a Bach flower remedy available in health food stores) in the dog's water or rubbing a few drops on the dog's gums can provide a calming effect. More recent research shows promise that D.A.P., a synthetic chemical that mimics the pheromone released when female dogs nurse their puppies, helps to calm stressed or anxious canines. D.A.P. can be used as a spray mist (on bedding, in a crate, etc.) or as a diffuser in the dog's room.

A safe place. It can be helpful to some Shih Tzu to provide a comfortable, safe place for the dog to curl up in when he's frightened. Solid, plastic crates with comfy bedding and just enough room (stand up, turn around, lie down) are usually coziest. For a crate to be a safe haven for a frightened Shih Tzu, however, you'll need to acclimate your Shih Tzu to a crate (see "Acclimation to the Carrier," page 116).

Medication. In severe cases in which the dog may become so frantic as to injure himself, consult with your veterinarian regarding medications that may calm your Shih Tzu. Many of these meds require

that the dog be dosed *prior* to the event (once the dog is upset, the medication won't calm him). Predicting when an event might occur (e.g., a thunderstorm) can be difficult.

Professional help. Maybe the problem is deeper than the sound itself. If you are having serious issues with your Shih Tzu, ask your veterinarian for a referral to a veterinary behaviorist, a veterinarian who has a special interest in behavior, or a skilled animal behaviorist. All of these professionals may be able to review your dog's situation and assist you in helping your Shih Tzu become more comfortable.

63

Working with the Adopted Dog

One of the biggest challenges to owning an adopted dog is helping him adjust to everyday sights and sounds. While many a rescued Shih Tzu has trotted right through the front door and into his new home, taken a look around, and behaved as if he'd lived there all his life, other rescues take more time. Often, the dog that is given up to rescue has not been well taken care of and hasn't had a lot of in-home time. But this isn't a reason to avoid the adopted Shih Tzu. If the dog has a nice temperament (and breed rescues don't place ill-tempered dogs), once he trusts you, he will usually adapt quite quickly to whatever life throws his way.

When working with a rescued Shih Tzu be aware that your adopted dog may have some unexpected anxieties. A ceiling fan may be cause for frenzied barking, for example, or turning on a garden hose outside may make your Shih Tzu run for cover. Not knowing your rescued dog's background can lead to some interesting surprises. To help your rescued Shih Tzu adjust to everyday life, follow the tips for working with puppies presented earlier in this chapter.

Go slowly and calmly with your adult dog. If you have any concerns contact the rescue group. These folks have lots of experience and are tremendous resources.

Easing Separation Anxiety

Most Shih Tzu don't like to be left alone. They're people dogs and prefer to go everywhere with you. There are times, of course, when your Shih Tzu needs to stay home alone. Though he may not like it, and may cry or whine a bit in protest, the well-adjusted Shih Tzu settles down quickly once you've left.

The Shih Tzu with separation anxiety behaves very differently. This dog doesn't settle down; rather, he becomes increasingly anxious while often displaying destructive behaviors. True separation anxiety can range from mild symptoms to such severe behaviors that the Shih Tzu may injure himself. Symptoms of separation anxiety include panting, drooling, pacing, destructive chewing, scratching, and/or urination/defecation within 30 minutes of your leaving the home.

It's natural for your Shih Tzu to miss you; however, extremely anxious Shih Tzu can hurt themselves in your absence and may experience separation anxiety.

Moderate to Severe Cases

If your Shih Tzu is suffering from separation anxiety, there are a few things you can do to help lessen his stress. First, change your routine of "leaving." Do you always grab your keys and a jacket before you walk out the house? Do you turn off lights? Shut a back door? Your Shih Tzu may know your routine better than you and likely has these movements tied into your leaving. When he sees you doing these things, he starts to get nervous. To prevent this from happening, change your routine so that you never perform the same sequence of actions when you leave.

Second and perhaps most importantly, begin randomly performing the actions of leaving throughout the day without leaving your home. Pick up your keys and then set them back down. Put on your jacket and then put it back. Close the back door and then open it again. As you work with your Shih Tzu, watch for good behaviors and reward them. Is his tail up and wagging when you grab your keys? What a good boy!

Third, you can try redirecting your Shih Tzu with another activity. For example, if your Shih Tzu has a particular toy he

loves or a chewie he likes, give him the special item, pick up your keys, put your keys back down, and then pick up the special item. He will begin associating the special treat with the sounds and actions that previously made him nervous and anxious.

Try to arrange your schedule so that you don't leave the house without your Shih Tzu for several weeks. Desensitizing your Shih Tzu to leaving requires that he no longer associates the signs of leaving with you actually departing the house.

For most people taking off from work for several weeks is just not possible. If this is the case, make arrangements for a trusted relative, neighbor, or pet sitter to come over before you leave for work. This distracts the dog when you leave the house. Another great alternative (and one that has the added benefit of distracting your dog with something very fun), is to sign up your Shih Tzu for a few weeks of doggie daycare.

Consult with your veterinarian regarding the possibility of using over-the-counter products (such as Rescue Remedy or D.A.P.), or a prescription medication to help your dog with his anxiety.

Finally, give the process time to work. Some behaviorists feel that even the most severe cases of separation anxiety can be cured or well-managed within six weeks. Granted, it can be a painfully involved six weeks on the part of the owner, but the results are generally permanent and well worth it—both financially (scratched doors, chewed furniture, ripped upholstery, and soiled rugs are expensive to replace!) and emotionally for both you and your dog.

TZU TIP

To determine if your Shih Tzu has separation anxiety, set up a tape recorder or a camcorder to hear or see exactly what your Shih Tzu is doing. If the behaviors stop a few minutes after you've left, your dog does not have separation anxiety.

Home Schooling

Nail Clipping and Other Everyday Necessities

Everyday grooming of your dog requires some work on your part; however, it's well worth the extra time. In addition to keeping your dog healthy (and spotting any abnormalities more quickly), you'll also save on some grooming fees and develop a deeper bond with your dog.

Nail Clipping

Being able to clip a puppy's or adult dog's toenails seems to be a difficult task for many pet owners, but every owner should be able to do so.

To get your Shih Tzu comfortable with nail clipping, try holding him in your lap (or on the grooming table), pick up a paw, praise your dog, and give him a treat. If he's okay with you touching his feet, you can then try to tap a nail ever so lightly with the clipper. Praise good behavior and give treats. If he begins getting restless, quit on a good note.

When your Shih Tzu's comfortable with you tapping his nails, you can then clip one. (Depending on how you have your Shih Tzu clipped, separating the nail from the paw's hair can take more time than a fidgety dog is willing to allow. If the hair on the paw is damp, it is much easier to see the nail and give it a quick trim.) With fussy pups or frightened adults, try to clip one nail a session. If all nails are nice and short, continue working with paw holding

and nail tapping each day. The more you handle your Shih Tzu's feet, the quieter he will be when you are clipping his nails.

Brushing

With a puppy coat, little brushing is required. However, if you plan on maintaining a full coat on your Shih Tzu, it's important to get him used to brushing—and lots of it. By the time his coat grows in, he'll be conditioned to stand or lie still long enough for you to work through the coat every day.

With a puppy, most of the grooming battle is getting him to be still for longer than a nanosecond. To combat this, introduce your puppy to his daily brushing when he's tired and about ready to nap. (This works for older dogs unaccustomed to daily brushing, too.) You can expect your Shih Tzu to be quieter and relax more readily when his body is naturally set to fall asleep.

Also, limit the time periods that you work on his coat. Start off with just a few minutes at a time; you may need several small sessions each day to get the job done. Work toward getting your Shih Tzu to tolerate 20 to 30 minutes of brushing everyday even if he doesn't need it with the clip he's currently in. This will get your Shih Tzu used to the grooming he'll need to be able to tolerate later.

Knots, mats, and tangles do hurt and they tend to occur in the most sensitive areas, particularly in the dog's armpit. Use detangling spray and work the tangle as best you can with your fingers and de-matting combs—without pulling on the hairs. If you are too rough with your brushing, your Shih Tzu will associate pain with brushing, which is not what you want.

Wash and Blow Dry

Breeders of show dogs recommend bathing your Shih Tzu puppy every Friday night and blowing him dry. Why? It's not that he needs to be bathed this frequently (this requires a very gentle dog shampoo that won't dry out a dog's coat or skin). Rather, it's that the show dog needs to be acclimated to the pre-show routine.

If you want your Shih Tzu to happily allow you to bathe and blow him dry, you need to practice more often than once every couple of months. Acclimating a puppy or dog to bathing is usually fairly simple: keep the water pleasantly warm but not hot, make sure you use a nonskid surface underfoot so he doesn't slip, and wash him gently, praising for good behavior. Avoid getting any water in the nose—it terrifies them when they can't breathe.

Blow drying your Shih Tzu can be a little scary because of the noise but it is necessary with a longer coat. Start your Shih Tzu off by turning on the blow dryer in the same room as you feed him treats. Your goal is to get him to associate the sound of the blow dryer with good things.

Work to move the source of the sound closer to the dog. Eventually, you'll want to be able to use the blow dryer on your Shih Tzu. Start low and work your way up his body, being careful not to hold the dryer in one spot for too long as this may burn the skin (resulting in hair falling out in that area). Avoid his head and try to keep him comfortable. Use lots of treats, lots of praise for good behavior, and lots of pats. Use a blow dryer designed for dogs; human blow dryers get far too hot for a dog's skin.

Acclimating to bath time is important to prevent future struggles.

Teeth

Dental care in toy breeds is particularly important. Shih Tzu are prone to build tartar on their back molars due to the angle of their jaws. If you have a puppy, you have the perfect opportunity to start off on the right tooth, so to speak. Begin brushing with a finger brush and toothpaste made specifically for dogs. Dogs can't spit, so human toothpastes are dangerous for them. Dog toothpastes also are made to taste good, so good, in fact, that brushing with the paste can be a reward for sitting still.

Once you've got your Shih Tzu adjusted to the finger brush (which you simply move back and forth gently all over his teeth), you can advance to a tooth brush. Of course, both finger brushes and toothbrushes can be seen as great chew toys, so do be patient with chewy puppies and careful with adult dogs if you haven't built up enough trust to confidently and safely stick your finger in his mouth.

7 *Basic Training Principles*

Anyone can train a dog and anyone can train a Shih Tzu. How quickly your dog learns, how many behaviors, commands, and tricks your Shih Tzu knows, how much fun he has, and how reliably he performs these skills has everything to do with *how* you train your Shih Tzu. Using the right equipment, the most enticing rewards, and keeping the work fun are all critical to success.

Equipment Essentials

When picking a training collar, the most important factors are that the collar fits comfortably, doesn't rub your Shih Tzu's lovely coat, and is functional.

There are quite a few different types of collars on the market that can be used for training—and each style has its unique benefits and potential drawbacks. Knowing how each type of collar functions will help you decide what collar to purchase for your Shih Tzu.

Buckles and Plastic Clip Closure Collars

The two simplest collars for training are the buckle collar and the adjustable-fit collar with a plastic clip closure (similar to the type of closure you would find on a life jacket). These collars can be made from a number of materials, including leather and cotton or nylon webbing. The collars come in varying widths but generally are fairly thin (½ inch to ⅝ inch) in smaller sizes.

The wider the collar, the less pressure it puts on your dog's neck. For example, a ¾-inch collar puts less pressure on the Shih Tzu's neck when he pulls than a ½-inch collar or a thin show lead. It doesn't take much pressure (or an accidental yank) to injure a Shih Tzu's vertebrae. Go gentle. Purchase the widest collar that's comfortable for your Shih Tzu.

Cotton and nylon webbed dog collars are washable and are relatively inexpensive. If your puppy or adult accidentally finds the collar and chews on it, a webbed collar isn't going to break the bank to replace. Leather collars can be pricier; however, the rolled styles are quite gentle on a Shih Tzu's coat.

A potential downside to both buckle and plastic clip collars is that because of the collar's limited size range, you may find that if you own a puppy, you will need to purchase more than one collar your first year to accommodate your growing Shih Tzu.

You should be able to fit two fingers between your dog's collar and his neck.

To fit a buckle or clip collar correctly, the collar should be snug (two fingers should fit between the collar and your dog's neck) and rest higher on the dog's neck, roughly right below the back of his ears. If the collar is too big, it is likely to pop right off your Shih Tzu's head if he makes an evasive, ducking maneuver.

Martingale Collars

A martingale collar is designed to be loose around the dog's neck when walking on a slack leash, but tightens to prevent the collar from popping off the dog's head if he suddenly pulls backwards. It can be quite narrow (the ½- to 2-inch rolled nylon style is often seen in the show ring) to wide (1 to 2 inches or wider). The wider collar is often referred to as a sighthound collar.

The martingale typically has D-rings on either side of the piece that lies across the dog's throat. A thin webbing runs

Shih Tzu are a joy to train!

through both of these D-rings and fastens together, forming a moving triangle, that tightens or loosens the collar. The leash attaches to the corner of the triangle with another ring.

When the throat piece is wide, the martingale is a very gentle collar and is quite comfortable for the dog. However, because of the extra loops and the manner in which the collar loosens around the dog's

neck, it can easily become caught on something. For this reason, the martingale collar should only be used when the Shih Tzu is supervised.

Slip Collars and Choke Chains

The training collars of choice for many years were metal linked choke chains and nylon slip or training collars. These consist of a length of linked chain or rolled nylon with rings on both ends. The length of collar is dropped through one of the rings to form a loop that tightens when the other ring is pulled with the leash.

A "pop" on the leash causes a "correction"—a quick tightening and release of the collar. A slip or choke collar is not necessary to train a Shih Tzu and is not recommended.

Harnesses

A harness takes all pressure off a dog's neck. The leash attaches to a ring located on the top of the harness, usually between the dog's shoulder blades or a little farther back. The well-fitted harness

is nearly impossible for a Shih Tzu to wriggle out of because both front legs are in the harness. Also, you can give your dog a little tug to get his attention without ever worrying about harming the vertebrae in his neck.

Harnesses can be a good choice for relaxed walking, dog park play, and informal training. With a harness, it's important that the fit is correct so that it is comfortable for the dog and doesn't pinch or pull anywhere. Harnesses can also rub and break your dog's coat hairs, so make sure this isn't an issue if you're trying to maintain a full coat.

Head Halters

Head halters work much like a halter and lead rope work with horses. The body follows where the head is being led. Canine head halters help dogs learn not to pull when walking. If the dog pulls hard while wearing a head halter, he whips around and finds himself facing you. Not what he had in mind!

A head halter fits with a piece that goes behind the dog's ears and another piece that goes over the muzzle. The two pieces fasten under the chin and the leash attaches at this junction under the chin.

The Shih Tzu is considered a brachycephalic breed and has a very short muzzle with large eyes. Fitting a Shih Tzu correctly with a head halter can be difficult; there's just not much nose for the halter to sit on. Some companies have created head halters specifically for brachycephalic breeds; however, the only way to know if it will work for your dog

is to have someone (preferably a trainer who has used these head halters before) to help you fit your Shih Tzu.

Leashes

A leash is a leash is a leash, right? Pretty much. The only leash qualities that need to be considered for training are length and materials.

You can purchase leashes ranging from four to six feet in length. Four feet is a nice training length; you won't have as much leash to juggle when your dog is working closely next to you. Six feet is a good length for walks; it allows a little more distance between you and your Shih Tzu. If your Shih Tzu doesn't walk nicely on a leash, it will be easier to work with him on a four-foot leash initially. Consider

TZU TIP

Retractable leashes, when in the unlocked position, allow a dog to reel out a cord or ribbon anywhere from six to 30 feet. These leashes are great in unfenced areas such as an unpopulated beach or park because they allow the dog to zing in and out at will. The leash is not good for training because it doesn't offer you enough control and it is bulky to hold. If you use one with a cord for recreational purposes, keep in mind that once your dog is out on the full length of leash, unless he wants to come back to you, it will be difficult to pull him back in. The cording will burn or cut your hands if you try to physically "reel in" your dog.

Some Shih Tzu are ball crazy and can be rewarded with toys rather than treats.

Using Reinforcements

Every dog and every handler is different. What works for one dog may not work at all for another. Therefore, a key aspect of using a positive, reward-based approach to dog training is figuring out just what motivates your Shih Tzu and reinforces good behavior.

Primary Reinforcement

When working with dogs, you'll hear the terms "primary" and "secondary" reinforcements. A primary reinforcement is the ultimate reward for a behavior that you want the dog to perform. The primary reinforcement appeals to the dog's natural desires or needs. Physical praise (pats, rubs, etc.) from the dog's special person are generally considered the most highly desirable of rewards. Verbal praise is always good but not as high up on the list as physical praise. With verbal and physical praise, you need to be careful not to overwhelm a less confident dog with too high a voice level or too physical a rubdown.

the six-foot leash a graduation present to a Shih Tzu who is pleasant to walk!

When choosing a leash for a puppy, you'll want the thinnest leash possible, with the smallest and lightest weight clip you can find. There's nothing worse than a heavy brass clip banging into your puppy's head! Nylon and cotton leashes, as well as leather, are all lightweight when in thin widths.

You can pick a slightly heavier leash for a larger adult dog; a ½-inch leash may not be comfortable in your hands when a 12-pound Shih Tzu decides to start chasing butterflies, oblivious to the fact that you're holding the other end of the leash. If your hands are sensitive, choose a leash made of soft cotton webbing as opposed to nylon, and pick a style that has a padded hand loop.

Food is another good primary reinforcement. Rewarding with delectable treats, particularly if the puppy or dog is a wee bit hungry, can be very motivational for a Shih Tzu. Food doesn't work if a dog isn't hungry, however, or if the dog or puppy is very nervous or anxious.

For the Shih Tzu with an exceptionally high prey or play drive, a special squeaky toy, tug toy, or a ball may be the best reward in the world. Narcotics detection

Secondary Reinforcement

A primary reinforcement is something that the dog naturally finds highly desirable. In other words, you don't have to teach a dog to want food, adore pats, or play with a favorite toy. They just do.

A secondary reinforcement is something that wouldn't necessarily be seen by your dog as a reward. Rather, it is something that the dog learns or is conditioned to recognize as a reinforcement. The dog recognizes the secondary reinforcement as positive because you—the trainer—link the primary or ultimate reward with the secondary reinforcement.

Examples of commonly used secondary reinforcements are a voice marker (a

dogs and police patrol dogs are often rewarded with a beaten-up, slobbery-looking tennis ball. These dogs are generally breeds with a very high prey/play drive. Since the Shih Tzu is not a breed known to be an insatiable retriever or one that goes particularly nuts over tugs and balls, a toy may produce only mild interest. If this is the case, go for the reward that produces a stronger response.

Every dog is different. Play around with your Shih Tzu to find out what his greatest driving force is—what he prizes the most of all. Don't be afraid to combine more than one primary reinforcement either, such as physical and verbal praise, food and pats, or food and praise. Find out what your Shih Tzu will work the hardest for and you've got a winning "primary" reinforcement.

A cute behavior can be reinforced with treats, and when linked with a command, turned into a trick.

Shih Tzu bore easily with repetitive training, so be sure to break up your exercises during the day.

simple exclamation, such as "Yes!"), a hand clicker (this requires a little coordination at first but most humans can be trained), or a sound, such as a cluck. To train the secondary reinforcement, you say the word or click the clicker and then treat your dog (if food is your primary reinforcement). It won't take long and your Shih Tzu will make the association between the secondary reinforcement and the highly desirable reward.

The beauty of using secondary reinforcements is that your dog will know he did something correctly and that the big treat is coming, but it doesn't have to come after every correct behavior.

In the initial training stages of any new behavior (*sit, down, stay*, etc.), you'll want to give the secondary and primary reinforcements after every correct repetition. As your Shih Tzu progresses in his training, you'll give the primary reward a little less often or after a series of correct behaviors.

Repetition

With dog training, practice doesn't make perfect; perfect practice makes perfect. Two things are important when you are training your Shih Tzu. First, set up the exercise so that your Shih Tzu has almost no possibility of failing. In other words, his probability of doing what you want him to do is much higher than his doing something else or becoming confused. This is called "setting your dog up for success."

Second, repeat the exercise so that the dog's successes far outnumber any slow, hesitant, or incorrect responses. Your goal is to get your Shih Tzu to perform the exercise with confidence eight out of ten times before making the exercise slightly more difficult.

An example of how this works can be seen in teaching the *sit* command. You will lure your Shih Tzu into the *sit* and then say, "Sit." He can't fail! He's already sitting when you give him the command. With repetition, your Shih Tzu will begin associating the word "Sit" with the sitting position.

Your next step is to make the exercise slightly harder by saying "Sit" just as his haunches are almost on the floor. Again, he almost can't fail. There is a slight possibility that the puppy or dog may pop back up before he completely sits, but if he's following a lure into the position, it's unlikely.

Repeat the exercise at least ten times before saying "Sit" a little sooner. Get the idea? It sounds slow, but it's really not. Repetition helps to solidify what the Shih Tzu is learning.

Don't make the mistake of focusing on an exercise for too long. Your pup will need to complete the exercise correctly and confidently for at least eight of ten repetitions, but you don't have to do all ten reps at once. Break them up throughout the day or over several days. It works—and quick, fast training sessions keep the excitement level up for the dog.

Keeping It Fun (The Art of Never Knowing It's Training)

Does your puppy get excited when you pull out a favorite squeaky toy for some one-on-one play? Does your older dog go bananas when he sees you reach for his leash to go on a walk? That's the reaction you want when you pull out your Shih Tzu's training collar. You want training to be the most fun activity of all.

Think of ways to make training exciting for your Shih Tzu. Keep it short. Keep it fast. Keep it interesting. And most importantly, make your Shih Tzu feel like he's the most important thing in your life in that moment. You'll be amazed what he will do!

When Not to Train

If you're in a bad mood, have had an exhausting day, or aren't feeling well, don't train. You'll wind up being impatient with your pup and the training session will go downhill from there. No one says you have to train according to a set schedule. Only train when it's optimal for both you and your Shih Tzu.

Likewise, if you're having a great day but your Shih Tzu is really struggling (and the training session is going nowhere quickly), switch to an exercise that is easy for your Shih Tzu to do. Reward him, have a crazy little play session, and quit.

Pick up your next training session with some fun, easy exercises for your Shih Tzu

When training in grass, make sure the grass is dry and hasn't been freshly mowed, unless you want a green Shih Tzu.

and see where it goes. It's far better to have fun and reinforce some easy exercises with your Shih Tzu (which will boost his confidence) than to push him too fast and too hard. It may take just a few just-for-fun sessions before your Shih Tzu is ready for something new, or it may take

several days. That's okay. He'll take off in another learning spurt soon. If he plateaus for a while, it's likely that he wasn't as confident and solid in his exercises as you might have thought. Time, patience, and keeping it fun for him will help him bump it up to the next level.

Training Clubs

You *can* train your dog yourself. Have confidence! You know your dog better than anyone else and even if you've never trained a dog before, you will figure out what works and what doesn't work with your Shih Tzu. As long as you keep things exciting, set realistic goals (people often expect too much too soon from their pups), and laugh a lot, you'll do great.

With that said, there are many benefits to joining a good training club. You will still do the bulk of your training with your Shih Tzu on your own; the training club will provide a safe setting for socialization and the opportunity to glean new training techniques and hands-on tips from top trainers. You'll be reassured that most of your problems with your Shih Tzu aren't really problems per se, but typical dog behaviors that are easily modified. And, if you do have an unusual or difficult issue you're dealing with, you're in the right place to get the help you need.

It's also fun to train with other people and their dogs. You'll be introduced to new and different dog activities, you'll see how talented your Shih Tzu really is, and

As a coated, brachycephalic breed, be careful of the heat when training your dog.

may find yourself interested in a sport that you'd never considered before.

How to Find a Great Training Program

Not all training programs are created equal. Opportunities for training classes and puppy programs are everywhere—you can find sign-ups for classes in malls, pet stores, shelters, and private training facilities. Prices range from nominal to exorbitant and trainers range from not-so-skilled to highly accomplished. Some trainers are terrific with Shih Tzu and others aren't, regardless of their credentials.

When searching for a good training class or club, visit a class or two, talk to trainers, and look for the following:

■ A clean facility (floors must be sanitized before puppy classes).
■ A club that insists on proof of vaccinations.
■ Participants who are having fun (that includes dogs and owners).
■ A program based on positive, reward-based training.
■ A small or toy breed class or classes in which small dogs are separated from large and super-sized breeds, and/or those with high prey drives.
■ Trainers who are friendly, easy to talk to, and experienced. A successful Shih Tzu trainer or someone who has trained multiple dogs and/or multiple owners with varying breeds to multiple titles is ideal. If the trainer doesn't

compete, he should have accreditation with a recognized organization that requires testing for certification, such as the Association for Pet Dog Trainers.
■ Trainers who are open to new training techniques and are flexible in conforming their training methods to fit your Shih Tzu, not the other way around.

When evaluating a trainer, a training club, or facility, trust your instincts. If it feels good and it's fun for you and your dog, you're in the right place. You don't have to be an experienced dog trainer to sense when something is right for you or your Shih Tzu. If you get an uneasy feeling that something isn't right—it probably isn't.

You must be comfortable with the trainer, the training methods, and the location and condition of the training facility. If it's not a good fit, keep looking until you find something that *does* work for you and your Shih Tzu.

Agility clubs have all the necessary equipment for training, saving you the expense of building your own obstacles.

Home Schooling

Figuring in the Caloric Count of Treats

A distinct downside to working with a toy breed is that too many treats can create chubby Shih Tzu. Obesity is a serious problem in dogs and one that you want to avoid ever having to deal with; keeping a Shih Tzu slim is much easier than trying to slim down an overweight dog.

If you do a lot of training with your Shih Tzu and you use food treats as lures and as rewards, you could be feeding your puppy or dog nearly his entire caloric requirements in four or five short training sessions.

There are two problems with this. One, if you feed your dog his regular food on top of all the treats, he is getting way too many calories each day and will quickly pack on weight. Two, if you cut back on his regular food to compensate for the increase in calories from the treats, you are most likely cutting out vital nutrition; your Shih Tzu's diet is now unbalanced. Neither situation is good.

So what can you do if you want to continue using training treats and keep your Shih Tzu's diet in check? You can look into low-calorie treats, portioning meals, or develop a diet that incorporates the use of training treats, yet is balanced and complete.

Low-Calorie Options

Raw veggies are great, low-calorie training treats. Diced carrots, tiny pieces of raw broccoli, slivers of squash, and chopped green beans are all healthy and contain few calories.

Of course, the only issue with these healthy snacks is that your dog has to want to eat them. Remember the importance of finding a primary reinforcement that literally drives your puppy or adult Shih Tzu mad? Most dogs will go ape for garlic chicken, cooked liver, or microwaved hotdog bits, but it takes a hungry Shih Tzu to crave raw veggies so much that they are the ultimate food reward. If you're concerned with your dog's weight gain, however, it is very much worth a try to see if your Shih Tzu will work for veggies.

A nervous dog may not be interested in treats and may work better with gentle praise.

Portioning Meals

If your Shih Tzu loves his food—and you're feeding him dry kibble (this won't work with wet food)—you can portion your dog's food into your training pouch.

So, for example, if you feed your Shih Tzu one and one half cups of dry kibble, take a half cup out of this portion each day and put it into your training pouch. Feed the remaining cup to your Shih Tzu in his regular meals. Use the kibble in your training pouch throughout the day for treats and rewards.

The obvious pitfall of this method is if your Shih Tzu doesn't see his regular food as anything "special." If this is the case, you won't be able to lure him into position with the food or use the food as a reward.

Developing a Diet

If you need to cut back on your dog's meals to compensate for training treats, you can make sure the ensuing treat/

diet combination meets your dog's nutritional needs by consulting with a board-certified veterinary nutritionist. Sadly these veterinarians are few and far between, but you can also access the Web site: *www.BalanceIt.com*. Designed by a board-certified veterinary nutritionist, this site allows pet owners to enter in some basic information about their dogs (age, sex, weight, etc.), plug in information about his regular food, and then add in the food that is being used as training treats.

The program then tells you if your dog's diet is balanced. If it's not, the program tells you how to correct the diet. If supplements are needed, the program tells you exactly which vitamins, minerals, and trace elements are needed and in what quantities.

If you make your Shih Tzu a home-cooked or raw diet, you can plug in the exact ingredients and the precise measurements you use in mixing your food to find out if you are meeting his nutritional requirements.

8 *Five Basic Commands*

The basic commands—*name*, *sit*, *stay*, *come* and *walk nicely*—are often all that many owners will need to enjoy living with a Shih Tzu. Whether you stop with the "fave five" or go on to teach additional skills to your dog (or even consider participating in agility or another sport), is up to you. Be forewarned, however, that many Shih Tzu owners find training so much fun that they go on to teach their Shih Tzu many more commands and a host of tricks.

Timing Behavior

With positive reward-based training, when you give a command to your dog is as important as when you reward the behavior. Timing is everything. Give a command or reward at the wrong time during an exercise, you wind up shaping the wrong behavior. For example, if you are in the beginning phases of teaching the *sit* and you say "Sit!" before the dog's haunches are squarely planted on the floor, you've just taught the "squat."

To avoid inadvertently teaching the wrong behavior or confusing the dog, begin by giving the command *as* the dog completes the behavior. As your Shih Tzu completes the correct position (or displays the correct behavior), mark the behavior with a verbal or mechanical signal (a clicker).

Marking is a bit redundant at the very beginning stages of training because it follows right on the heels of the command. However, as your dog progresses to receiving the command first and following with the behavior, the mark becomes critical to precisely identify when the dog is correct.

The reward (a treat, praise, pats, a toy, etc.) follows the mark. After the reward comes the release command such as "Okay" or "All done!" Though it sounds like overkill to have a release command, you'll be surprised how often a Shih Tzu will remain in position until you tell her she's finished. Repeat the process to help solidify what your dog has just learned.

Sound confusing? It's really not, once you get the hang of it. In fact, a lot of this sequence happens quite naturally—it's just that the things you may already have been doing now have a name. Putting it all together, here's how the entire training sequence goes:

1. **Behavior.** Lure the dog into position using a treat as a guide (lure shaping) or wait until the dog shows the behavior independently on his own (free shaping).

2. **Command.** Say the command when the dog is in the correct position or performing the desired behavior.
3. **Mark.** Mark the correct behavior with a verbal "Yes!" or mechanical signal (a click from a clicker) so the dog knows precisely when he is correct.
4. **Reward.** Reward the behavior with a treat, play with a ball, tug on a towel, etc. followed by the ultimate reward of physical praise (pats and rubs).
5. **Release.** Release your Shih Tzu from the position or behavior with a command, such as "Okay!"
6. **Repeat.** The generally accepted idea is that a dog should complete the exercise correctly 8 to 10 times with confidence, before the exercise is made any more difficult.

Name

Teaching a puppy or dog to respond instantly when you say his name is not only helpful in the home, it is an excellent way to set up your dog to pay close attention to what is coming next. In many instances, this will be a command or some sort of direction from you.

Free-Shaping Name

You can teach *name* in one of several ways. With free shaping, wait until your Shih Tzu is looking directly and intently at you. Say the dog's name. Mark ("Yes!" or click), reward (treat, praise), and release ("Okay!"). With this method, you can't repeat the exercise ten times in a row, because you'll need to wait until you

Most Shih Tzu are eager to learn commands, especially when training resembles play.

"catch" your puppy looking at you again. If you pay attention, you'll find multiple opportunities throughout the day to free-shape *name*.

Once you are getting recognition from your Shih Tzu, the next step would be to say the dog's name as the dog begins to look at you—at this point looking at you is virtually a given. After this is performed successfully many times throughout the day, then you can say the dog's name when he is not quite looking at you, but not distracted. At this point, you can begin

Saying "down" now would teach a *crouch* instead of a *down*.

repetitions because your Shih Tzu has made the association between his name and turning his complete attention to you.

Lure-Shaping Name

Another way to teach *name* is to use a food lure.

1. With a treat in one hand and the other relaxed at your side, show the dog the treat; pull the treat up to your chin.
2. Say the dog's name.
3. When he responds by looking at your face, mark ("Yes!" or a click).
4. Reward (give the dog the treat that you are holding).
5. Release ("Okay!").
6. Repeat.

As your puppy or dog learns his name and looks to you for what's next, you can begin to fade out the treats. Fading means that the dog will eventually be rewarded with a treat (or a ball, if he's toy crazy) but won't receive the reward every time. He may have to perform several repetitions to earn the treat—or with more advanced training, perform several different exercises.

Sit

The value of a good, solid *sit* can't be overrated. Does your Shih Tzu have a

When your Shih Tzu is looking at you, say his name.

tendency to jump up on people as they come into your home? *Sit.* When it's time to eat dinner, does he put his paws up on the bowl as you're lowering it to the floor and knock it out of your hands? *Sit.* How about when it's time to go on a walk and he tries to bolt out the door? *Sit.*

The *sit* is also a wonderful tool to defuse poor behavior or to calm a really excited dog. If the dog is barking at another dog on a walk, for example, you can give the *sit* command, and reward the *sit*. The *sit* can also be used to catch a Shih Tzu that is running loose (and perhaps doesn't have a solid *come* in his repertoire as yet).

The *sit* is a great command that most Shih Tzu pick up very quickly. It's also easy to train.

Free-Shaping Sit

If your Shih Tzu sits frequently on his own, it's fairly easy to associate this behavior with the command *sit*. Keep a little bag of treats in your pocket and when you see your puppy or dog sit, say "Sit!" then mark, reward, release.

As with any other free-shaping exercise, you can't "repeat" because you must wait until the dog performs the behavior

Free-shape the *sit* by saying "Sit" whenever you spot your Shih Tzu sitting.

on his own. Keep those treats with you and every time you catch your dog sitting, say, "Sit!" and mark, reward, release.

As you see your dog making the command-behavior link, you can begin giving the command *just prior* to the dog's bum firmly planting on the floor.

Lure-Shaping Sit

With your Shih Tzu facing you, gently hold the dog's collar or harness with your left hand.

1. Holding a small, delectable treat in your right hand, slowly pass the treat from the tip of the dog's nose, back to his ears. The treat should just barely skim over the nose, bridge, and top of the head.
2. Your dog will rock back into a sit. Right as his rear end plants on the floor, say "Sit."

(1) Take a treat and move it slowly backwards.

(2) Say "Sit" as your Shih Tzu completes the *sit*.

3. Mark the behavior with a click or "Yes!"
4. Reward the behavior with the treat in your hand, praise, and some pats.
5. Release the dog with your release command, "Okay!"
6. Repeat until the dog is getting it right—and with confidence—for 8 to 10 repetitions. (Young puppies will not have the attention span to do this many repetitions in one sitting. It's fine to break up *sits* throughout the day with all ages of dogs.)

When your Shih Tzu has the idea, you can make it more difficult by giving the command as the treat is passing over the dog's head and the dog is folding into the *sit*. When this is mastered, try giving the command when the treat is in front of the dog's nose, and then without holding onto his collar. If you've been working on a table, try the same command with your Shih Tzu on the floor.

If at any time the dog seems confused or isn't completing 8 to 10 reps with confidence, go back a step, making multiple repetitions at the easier level until he's got it again.

TZU TIP

If leaning over to shape a sit is a strain for you, consider sitting or kneeling on the floor or raising the dog to your level by placing him on a rubber or non-slip mat on a wide table or grooming table.

Sit *with Hand Signals*

When your Shih Tzu is sitting on command without using the treat to shape the sit or you holding the collar to steady him, you can add a hand signal. It's a fun thing to teach your Shih Tzu to respond to commands without voicing them, and you can teach friends and children of all ages to give a hand signal to your dog. Sometimes the difference in people's enunciation of a command differs, as does the pitch of the voice (particularly with small children). The hand signal, however, is usually recognizable by the dog regardless of the person giving it.

The signal can really be anything you want. One simple movement is to take your left palm and raise it from your side to waist height, directly in front of you. Your forearm will be parallel to the floor, fingertips pointing toward the dog. Give the hand signal at the same time as the voice command.

Similar in concept to free-shaping, in which you apply the word with the behavior the dog is performing, the dog learns to associate the hand signal to the voice command. Dogs are visually oriented and pick up hand movements quickly. Remember to be consistent in whatever hand signal you choose.

After several days of combining the hand movement with the voice command, you can begin fading out the voice. Start with several repetitions of voice and hand signal together, then a hand signal only, then several combined reps, then a hand signal only. If a hand signal only doesn't provide an immediate *sit*, it is okay to say "Sit!" and, if necessary, use a treat to

An errant Shih Tzu that doesn't have a solid recall (yet) will often *sit* on command at a distance, giving you enough time to walk up to him and clip a leash on his collar.

shape the *sit*. However, if this happens, go back to combining the voice command with the hand signal for many more repetitions before attempting again to go voiceless.

TZU TIP

When using the free-shaping training method, be careful not to be too enthusiastic in your commands. You may distract your dog so much that he actually stops the behavior you want!

Stay

If the *sit* is a helpful command, *stay* makes the *sit* even more valuable. Imagine this: You're in the kitchen and you drop a drinking glass on the tile floor. Shards of glass are everywhere. Your Shih Tzu comes running in to investigate. *Sit! Stay!* Your sweet puppy comes to a skidding halt, sits down, and *stays*. "Good dog," you say as you go over to him, releasing him from the *sit-stay*, scooping him up and putting him in a crate while you safely clean up the mess. Whew! That was a close one.

Or, picture this: A frail neighbor comes to the door and your very excited Shih Tzu is running circles around the foyer. If you let your neighbor in, he will surely tumble over the dog. *Sit! Stay!* Now you can open the front door and let your neighbor in without any worries.

So, how does this incredible *stay* command evolve? It takes consistency, time, and patience.

1. With your dog on leash and at your left side, put your dog into a *sit*.
2. Holding the leash in your right hand, bend down and, with your left hand, give the *stay* hand signal (fingers together and pointing toward the ground with palm toward and directly in front of the dog's nose) while saying "Stay!"
3. Remain standing next to your dog for a few seconds, then mark, reward, release.
4. Repeat the exercise until your Shih Tzu stays in a *sit* for several seconds for 8 to 10 repetitions. (With young

puppies that can't want to stay still for very long, you can work on this exercise various times during the day rather than at one long stretch.)
5. Add time. Put your Shih Tzu in a *sit-stay* and have him sit quietly for 15 seconds. Then 20 seconds. Work up to a full minute.
6. Add distance. Put your Shih Tzu in a *sit-stay* and take one step to the right, step back, and immediately mark, reward, release, repeat. (When adding distance, the time variable goes back to just a few seconds.)
7. Try the same exercise with one step forward. Then one step backward. If your Shih Tzu moves, go back to being motionless next to him. Mark, reward, release, repeat.
8. Add time to the step away. Put your dog in a *sit-stay*, take a step to the right, stay there for several seconds and step back. Mark, reward, release, repeat.

To make the *sit-stay* increasingly difficult, you can walk to the end of the leash, walk completely around your dog, or attach two leashes together to increase the distance. If your dog breaks the *sit-stay*, put him gently back into a *sit* and repeat the *stay* command staying close by him for several seconds. Mark, reward, release. Go back to an easier level of the *sit-stay*

TZU TIP

With the stay, always step away from your dog on the right foot. When you want your dog to come with you, step out on your left foot. It's a subtle difference, but your dog will pick up on it.

(1) When your Shih Tzu is in a *sit*, give him the voice command and hand signal for *stay*.

(2) Take one step to the right.

(3) Immediately step back.

(4) Praise and release him!

and work back up to the level at which she was having trouble. Most likely, you may have rushed a step along the way.

It's wise to start any new command training in a quiet room in your home with no distractions. As your Shih Tzu begins to excel in a particular exercise, you can add distractions (have someone walk by, roll a ball, etc.). Always work with the simplest *sit-stay* first and then build up to the level at which your dog was performing prior to the addition of the distractions. Additional distractions can be added simply by moving outside to your front yard and then to busier locations, such as a small park or a wide sidewalk in front of a strip mall.

Remember, whenever going to a new location, keep the exercise very, very simple and build back up to the level at which your dog was previously working. You're trying to set your dog up for success with as many correct repetitions of an exercise as possible. Every time your dog doesn't get it "right" means more work for you and your dog at a lower level. Keep it fun and it will keep moving!

Come

Being able to call your dog and have him come running to you (or at the very least move in your direction at the pace of his

Adding distance, time, or distractions will make the *sit-stay* more difficult.

To free-shape the *come*, give the command when you know your Shih Tzu is already coming toward you.

choice) can truly be a lifesaver. The puppy that slips her leash on a busy sidewalk, or the dog that bolts out the front door happens to even the most vigilant of dog owners. A very scary "the-dog-is-loose moment" is inevitable at some point in a dog owner's life.

What if this happened and you couldn't call your dog back?

If you find yourself in this situation and you've worked diligently on the *come*, the odds are greatly in your favor that your dog will return when you call him.

Free-Shaping Come

One of the easiest ways to begin associating the *come* command with the dog coming to you is to wait until it happens. If you find your puppy or dog hurtling toward you, run back a few steps as he approaches and say, "Come!" Mark, reward, release.

From this initial word/behavior association, you can do things to try to initiate your dog to come to you. Say the dog's name, and then start trotting backwards. As soon as your puppy or adult starts to run towards you, say "Come!" Mark, reward, release.

To advance beyond these two levels of free-shaping, and to make sure that your Shih Tzu really doesn't have any opportunity to fail at the *come* command, it is best to begin working on-leash. When working on-leash, you can ensure that the dog comes to you. You can also add dis-

tance and distractions while working in many different locations.

On-Leash Come

There are several ways to practice the *come* command on-leash with your dog. Two of the best include a technique that is used while out on walks; the other is one that can be used with the Shih Tzu with a solid *sit-stay*.

On Walks
1. While walking your dog, stop and start trotting backwards. When your Shih Tzu whips around ("Where did you go? Oh, there you are!") and starts running toward you say, "Come!" Encourage your Shih Tzu to come quickly by making it a lot of fun—go backwards a little faster and verbally cheer him on. When he runs up to you, mark, reward, release.

(1) Walk forward briskly.

(2) Stop and walk backwards.

(3) The moment your Shih Tzu turns to change direction, too, say "Come!"

(4) Encourage him to run toward you as you trot backwards a few more steps.

2. Give the *come* command sporadically during all walks.
3. After several days of the *come* command on walks, try giving the command as soon as you start stepping backwards. Mark, reward, release.
4. Give the *come* command on walks when your Shih Tzu is sniffing at something in the grass (just make sure he's not sniffing because he needs to relieve himself). If he hesitates, take several steps backward. Mark, reward, release.

With the *Sit-Stay*

1. Put your Shih Tzu in a *sit-stay* and walk to the end of the leash, turn and face your dog.
2. Say *"Come!"* and jog a few steps backward. Encourage your Shih Tzu to come quickly with lots of enthusiastic encouragement.
3. When he reaches you, mark, reward, release, repeat.
4. When he has mastered this (8 to 10 reps that are consistent and performed with confidence and enthusiasm), you can make it a little more difficult. Add distance with a long line. Work in places other than your backyard or in the home—but when you do, go back to the simplest form of the *come*, which is just to the end of the leash. Build slowly from there.

Walk Nicely

The Shih Tzu is little. How hard can it be to walk this dog? You might be surprised! The issue for most adults is not how hard

---

TZU TIP

To get a faster recall, amp up the excitement. As your Shih Tzu comes toward you, turn around and start running away from him. That should get him excited! Or, surprise your dog by tossing a favorite toy between your legs as he runs toward you, letting him run through your legs to pounce on the toy.

the dog pulls (though if you have difficulties walking or have arthritis in your hands, this little dog *can* give a significant pull), but all the different directions the dog can go in a matter of seconds.

Puppies often prefer to chew on a leash, as opposed to being attached to one.

Backward, forward, left, right and then back again—oops, something interesting is over here, and so it goes. Without any leash training, you can forget any form of consistent forward motion on walks and had better be nimble on your feet, as well as adept at untangling your legs and arms from the leash.

If you'd prefer that your Shih Tzu trot alongside you while on walks, then teaching him to *walk nicely* is a very worthwhile endeavor.

1. Bring along treats or a favorite toy for your walk—you'll need them to help keep your dog's attention and as rewards.
2. Invest in a short leash. A four-foot leash will keep your Shih Tzu much closer than a six-foot leash.
3. Think in opposites. If your Shih Tzu forges ahead, walk backwards. If he pulls left, turn right. If he pulls right, turn left. (Your walk will look a little crazy at first and neighbors may begin to whisper, but this technique really does work to get—and keep—your dog's attention.)
4. Talk to him to keep his focus on you. Remember the name training you did? Say his name from time to time and treat him immediately for looking at you.
5. When he is walking beside you and paying attention, give him a treat.
6. If your Shih Tzu loves playing with a certain toy, take it along with you on your walk. Hold it in your right hand and walk briskly, swinging your hand so your puppy or adult gets an occasional glimpse of the toy. Reward nice walking with a play session.
7. Practice, practice, practice. It does, indeed, make (nearly) perfect!

Home Schooling

No "Repeat" Commands

A very common error among handlers is repeating a command. You know the routine: The dog *knows* he is supposed to sit when you say "Sit!" Until, of course, the day he spots something over at the edge of the fence and isn't paying attention. You repeat the command to get her attention. When the second command doesn't work, you say "Sit!" a bit more firmly.

This might work, but if it doesn't, you may let a fourth "Sit!" roll from your lips before your Shih Tzu decides it's time to *sit*.

What your pup has learned is that "Sit!" doesn't really mean *sit* until the fourth or fifth time. "Sit!" has now become "Sit. Sit, Sit, Sit, SIT!"

Say the command only once. If the dog doesn't provide the correct behavior, which in this instance is sitting, don't repeat the command. Instead shape the correct behavior with a treat. Now you can reward the dog for doing it right. Go back to the basics of shaping with a lure for several repetitions and bring the dog back to the level where he "ignored" your command.

Remember, if you have a non-response to a command, it is always the trainer's fault, never the dog's. You are most likely asking too much, too quickly from your Shih Tzu.

9 *Seven More Commands*

You and your Shih Tzu could probably survive just fine knowing a few, basic obedience commands. *Sit, stay, come,* and *walk nicely* are definitely the essentials to home-living. If you want an exceptionally easy Shih Tzu to live with, however, consider adding a few more commands to his repertoire. You might be surprised how easily the following commands can come in handy!

Down

The *down* is an excellent command to teach your Shih Tzu because it is helpful on many different levels. A solid *down* can be used to help a boisterous puppy or anxious adult dog to quietly settle himself. The *down* is a good command to use when answering the front door when you don't want your Shih Tzu jumping up on people, bolting out the open door, or barking. (It's difficult for a dog to bark while in the *down* position.)

Maybe you have a Shih Tzu who dances on his back legs to beg for food when you're eating? As cute as the dancing Shih Tzu is, this can elevate to pawing, scratching, and barking at mealtimes. *Down* keeps your Shih Tzu from becoming a pest and it's a position that he can maintain

comfortably for five, ten, fifteen minutes or longer. He may even fall asleep in his bed for a short nap!

Additionally, if your Shih Tzu has a tendency to be a bit pushy with family members, the *down* helps to gently assert leadership. Once your Shih Tzu is solid with his *down,* you can teach young family members how to give the command (with you present) to help ensure that the dog understands he is a treasured pet, not the boss of your children.

Lure-Shaping the Down

In this exercise, the *down* is shaped after the dog is in a *sit.* (You can also do this same exercise from a standing position.)

1. Put your Shih Tzu into a *sit.*
2. Move the treat from his nose slowly down to the floor.
3. As your Shih Tzu lies down with his elbows *completely* on the ground, say "Down."
4. Mark the behavior with a click or "Yes!"
5. Reward the behavior with the treat.
6. Release him from the *down* with your release command.
7. Reinforce his good behavior with some additional praise and pats.

8. Repeat the exercise until your Shih Tzu moves quickly and easily into the *down* following the food lure. (Remember, your initial goal is to get your Shih Tzu to perform 8 to 10 correct, confident, and quick *downs* using the lure. These repetitions should be spread out throughout the day and possibly over several days.)

Once your Shih Tzu has linked the word, "Down" with lying down, you can make the exercise a smidgeon more difficult. As you move the lure to the floor, say, "Down," just before he is completely down. You want him to be so close to lying down that it would be difficult for him to pop back up; he's more likely to lie down than sit or stand. When he is down, mark, reward, release, and reinforce his good *down* with more praise and pats.

When he's got this mastered (with confidence, speed, and enjoyment), say the command "Down" a little earlier. When he is down, mark, reward, release, and reinforce him with praise and pats. Your goal is to work toward being able to say the word "Down" and have your Shih Tzu eagerly plop into a solid *down*.

Once you can say "Down" and easily lure him to the floor, you can start luring him *less*. For example, start with the lure in front of his nose, but take it only halfway to the floor. Eventually, you'll want to be able to say "Down" without using the treat as a food lure at all.

If your Shih Tzu appears confused or hesitant at any time, make the exercise

> ### TZU TIP
> When working on luring the down, *don't* move the treat too closely to the Shih Tzu's chest. If you do his front end will go down, but his rear end will pop up. If you hold the lure too far in front of the Shih Tzu, he will break his sit and lunge for the treat. Be patient! It may take a little practice to find the perfect path for the food lure but you can make the down happen!

easier. Go back to fully luring him to the ground. After a few successful repetitions try cutting back on the food lure.

If your Shih Tzu has lots of energy and has a hard time focusing, try to help her burn off a little steam before she begins her training sessions.

(1) From a *sit*, move the treat slowly to the ground.

(2) It may take a little practice to get the treat in just the right place for your Shih Tzu to get *all* the way to the ground without bouncing back up.

Down *with* Hand Signals

Adding a hand signal to the *down* is pretty simple. Actually, the hardest part may be in choosing what hand signal to use.

Appropriate hand signals for a *down* include a simple finger point, a downward motion of the hand (as if you're pushing something down from your chest to your hip), a big, sweeping upward motion of your hand and arm (as if you're throwing a baseball over your shoulder), or a palms down, left to right movement of your hand, keeping your arm slightly bent and by your side.

Whatever hand signal you choose, be consistent.

To link the hand signal with the command, make sure your Shih Tzu is folding into his down reliably and with confidence. Then give the hand signal at the same time that you say "Down." Mark, reward, release.

Repeat the combination of hand signal and voice command for several days or however long it takes to combine the visual and verbal commands for roughly 20 to 30 repetitions. Once you've linked the hand signal with the voice command, try giving the hand and voice together for two repetitions and then immediately give the third repetition with the hand signal only. Mark, reward, release. Yay! He did it!

If your Shih Tzu hesitates or seems slow to go into the *down*, you haven't linked the visual and verbal commands well enough. Help him by giving the voice command for the *down*. Mark, reward, release. Then, go back to something that your Shih Tzu is more confident with. Ask for a *down* with the combined voice and hand signals for *down*. Mark, reward, release. Try using only the hand signal again after several reps of the two signals together. Again, these reps may be performed over a period of days; keep things fun.

Variation: **Down-Stay**

What's better than a Shih Tzu that drops into a *down* on command? A Shih Tzu that stays in a *down*! Teaching the *down-stay* is virtually identical to teaching the *sit-stay* (page 86), except, of course, your Shih Tzu is in a *down*.

The most important thing to remember when teaching the *stay* variation of any command is to only increase one variable of the exercise at a time. Increase these variables in very tiny increments. Remember, the whole idea is to set your Shih Tzu

Adding a hand signal to the *down* is easy.

up so he almost can't fail, at *each* level of the exercise.

Time, distance, leash/off-leash, and distractions are the variables of the *stay* command. When you increase or add a variable, *decrease* the other variables until your dog is confident he knows what he's doing.

An example of how you can teach the *down-stay* is as follows:

1. With your Shih Tzu on leash put him in a *down*.
2. Holding the leash in your right hand, bend down and give the *stay* hand signal (fingers together and pointing toward the ground, moving the palm toward and directly in front of the dog's nose) and the voice command "Stay."
3. Remain standing next to your dog for a few seconds, then immediately mark the *down-stay* with a click or "Yes!"

4. Reward the *down-stay* with a treat or verbal and physical praise.

5. Release the dog from the *down-stay* with "Okay!" or a *release* hands signal, such as a pat on the chest.

6. Repeat the exercise until your Shih Tzu remains down for several seconds for 8 to 10 repetitions. Remember to spread out these repetitions through two or more training sessions. Keep it bright and light!

7. Add time. Put your Shih Tzu in a *down-stay* and increase the amount of time he remains in the *down* by ten seconds. Mark, reward, release and complete 8 to 10 repetitions successfully over a period of training sessions. Add time in very small increments with young puppies and try to work on this exercise when your Shih Tzu is a little tired. He's more likely to stay in his *down*.

8. Add distance. Put your Shih Tzu in a *down-stay*. Take one step to the right and immediately step back. (The time variable goes back to zero.) Mark, reward, release, repeat.

9. Change directions. Put your Shih Tzu in a *down-stay*. Take one step forward on your right foot. (Stepping forward with your left foot is the signal to your dog that you want him to move forward.) Step back immediately. Mark, reward, release, repeat. Work toward being able to step out and back in any direction and even around your dog.

10. Combine variables. Remember, if you increase one variable (the time your Shih Tzu remains in a *down-stay*), then decrease another variable (the distance you stand away from your dog).

Off

Off is a good command for getting a comfort-seeking Shih Tzu to hop down from a couch, bed, or chair—especially one that he's not supposed to be lying on.

To get started—and to keep or reclaim your seat on the couch or pillow on the bed—here's how to approach teaching the *off* command.

1. Place your Shih Tzu on a low-level couch. (Never ask your Shih Tzu to jump from a high location. Use a step stool to allow him to gain access to allowable furniture.)

2. With treat in hand, lure him off the couch.

3. Say "Off!" when all four feet are on terra firma.

4. Mark the behavior with a click or "Yes!"

5. Reward the behavior with the food lure.

6. Reinforce the behavior with praise and pats.

7. Release with an "Okay" or a pat on the chest.

8. Repeat by putting him back up on the couch and going through steps 1 through 6 again. Practice a few times each day. Progress to being able to give the command without using the food lure.

TZU TIP

Only allow your Shih Tzu on furniture if it is very low or if you provide steps. Shih Tzu frequently receive serious injuries from jumping off or falling from couches and beds. Be sure to make getting up and down from furniture safe for your dog.

Though the Shih Tzu can easily be picked up and moved, teaching the *off* command helps to assert good leadership skills.

Add a hand signal. A good visual cue for this command is a finger snap followed by pointing to where you want the dog to go. Practice with the voice command and eventually wean to using just the snap and point hand signal.

Variation: **Move It!**

What if you don't mind your Shih Tzu up on the couch but you'd like him to move over a cushion to make room for you? You can teach the *move it* command, which is really just a variation of *off.* (If you've already taught your Shih Tzu the *off* command and have linked it with the snap and point hand signal, *move it* will be even easier.)

1. Place your Shih Tzu on the couch.
2. With treat in hand, lure him to the next cushion.
3. Say "Move it!" when he's on the next cushion.
4. Mark the behavior with a click or "Yes!"
5. Reward the behavior with the food lure.
6. Release the behavior—he can romp around the couch now; he doesn't have to stay on that cushion.
7. Reinforce the behavior with praise and pats.
8. Repeat by settling him down on the couch again (anywhere is fine) and then going through steps 1 through 7 again. Practice a little at a time, keep it fun, and progress to giving the command without using the food lure.

The outdoors can provide additional training distractions that you wouldn't normally find in the quiet of your home.

9. Add the hand signal. If you're asking your dog to move, snap and point your finger where you want him to go.

To keep the *move it* and *off* commands from becoming too structured (and boring), turn the snap and point hand signal into a game. How fast can your Shih Tzu move? How fast can he figure out where you're pointing? You can make learning this important skill into a game. Try using a toy as a lure and letting him play with the toy (and you) after your "training" session.

Stand

With all the grooming that is required of a Shih Tzu in a full coat, and even the daily needs of a Shih Tzu in a puppy clip, the *stand* command comes in handy. It's also a good command to have in your puppy's or dog's repertoire when he goes for veterinary exams.

If you have plan to compete in obedience or if you've purchased your Shih Tzu with a show contract and need to have him "ring ready" (for you or a handler), the *stand* is an important skill for both of these events. In the entry level in obedience (Companion Dog), one of the exercises a dog must pass is the "stand for examination." This is an abbreviated version of the show ring procedure, in which the judge looks at the dog's teeth, examines his bone structure, and feels the dog's conformation.

Whether using the stand for home or competitive purposes, you're bound to find some good uses for it.

1. Walk your Shih Tzu forward a few steps.
2. Slow to a halt, placing your hand gently under your dog's tuck up (the soft belly behind his ribs).
3. Say "Stand" while holding him gently in position for a few seconds. He should not move his feet.
4. Mark the behavior with a click or "Yes!"
5. Reward the behavior with the food lure.
6. Release him from his *stand* with "Okay!" You may also give a pat on the chest for a physical cue that he's finished with the exercise.
7. Reinforce the behavior with praise and pats.

(1) When your dog is standing, give him the *stand* command.

(2) Mark the behavior, release him, and give him a reward.

8. Repeat steps one through seven. Practice a few times each day.
9. Practice on the grooming table. Lift the dog up on the table, place his front paws near the edge and restrain him lightly. Go through steps 3 through 8. Repeat a few times a day.

Variation: **Stand-Stay**

The *stand* is not a naturally comfortable position for most dogs to hold for any length of time, nor is it a popular position for wriggly puppies. For these reasons, it is important to keep the *stand-stay* reasonable in both time (how long you expect your Shih Tzu to remain standing) and distance (how far away you stand from your dog).

Incorporate the *stay* into a solid *stand* command.

1. With your Shih Tzu on-leash walk forward and put him in a stand.
2. Holding the leash in your right hand, bend down and give the *stay* hand signal (fingers together and pointing toward the ground, moving the palm toward and directly in front of the dog's nose) and the voice command "Stay."
3. Remain standing next to your dog for a few seconds, then immediately mark the *stand-stay* with a click or "Yes!"
4. Reward the *stand-stay* with a treat or verbal and physical praise.
5. Release the dog from the *stand-stay* with a release command "Okay!" or a hand signal, such as a pat on the chest.

6. Repeat the exercise until your Shih Tzu is standing for several seconds for 8 to 10 repetitions. Remember to spread these repetitions through two or more training sessions. This is a hard exercise for most dogs.

7. Put your Shih Tzu in a *stand-stay* and increase the amount of time he remains in the *stand* by five seconds. Mark, reward, release, and complete 8 to 10 repetitions successfully over a period of training sessions.

8. Add distance. Put your Shih Tzu in a *stand-stay*. Take one step to the right and immediately step back. (The time variable goes back to zero.) Mark, reward, release, repeat.

9. Change directions. Put your Shih Tzu in a *stand-stay*. Take one step forward on your right foot. (Never step out with your left foot if you want your Shih Tzu to stay. Stepping forward with your left foot signals your dog to move forward with you.) Step back immediately. Mark, reward, release, repeat. Work toward being able to take a step in any direction and eventually to walk around your dog.

10. Combine variables. Remember, if you increase one variable (the time your Shih Tzu remains in a *stand-stay*), then decrease another variable (the distance you stand away from your dog).

Back

Teaching your Shih Tzu to *back* can come in handy, too.

Say you've walked in the front door, carrying an armload of groceries. Your Shih Tzu rushes the door and is jumping up in a mad, loving greeting. You need to move forward but can't because you can't see where your little guy is over the top of the grocery bags.

But hey! You've taught your Shih Tzu the *back* command. "Back," you tell your Shih Tzu and there he goes, backing up two or three feet. Out of your way, in your line of vision and no longer under foot. No groceries are dropped, no Shih Tzu is stepped on, and everyone is happy.

Here's how to teach this skill.

1. Put your Shih Tzu on-leash and stand to face him, with a wall to one side of both of you.

2. Slowly shuffle forward into your Shih Tzu.

3. If you keep him directly in front and facing you, he will need to step backward. The wall prevents him from swinging his rear end around and facing the other direction.

4. As soon as he takes a step backward, say "Back!"

5. Mark the behavior with a click or "Yes!"

6. Reward the behavior with a treat, praise, and pats.

7. Release the *back* with a release command ("Okay!") or a hands-on signal (pat on the chest).

8. Repeat the exercise, trying to get one or two steps backward each time. Work on the exercise sporadically through the week, trying to help your Shih Tzu associate "Back" with stepping backwards.

9. Work on getting your Shih Tzu to back more steps at a time. Then try backing without the help of the wall. Eventually he will back up without your walking into him.

Take It *and* Out

Shih Tzu are notorious for finding things to eat or chew that they aren't supposed to have. This habit is more than an annoyance. Some items can be extremely dangerous or even fatal if swallowed.

In an emergency, you don't want your Shih Tzu clenching his jaws and giving you a look of defiance! Teaching the *out* command will solve this problem.

The *out* command goes hand-in-hand with the *take it* command, so you may as well teach both at the same time.

1. Choose an item that is soft and easy for your Shih Tzu to hold, such as a small cuddle toy. The item should also be something that your Shih Tzu wants to hold or carries around the house naturally.
2. With your Shih Tzu on-leash (so he can't run off with the item), offer your puppy or dog the item.
3. When he takes it in his mouth, say "Take it!"
4. Mark the behavior with a click or "Yes!"
5. Reward the behavior with praise, pats, and rubs. (Don't offer him a treat yet. He'll drop the toy!)
6. Now offer him a treat and as he drops the toy to take it, say "Out!"
7. Mark the behavior with a click or "Yes!"
8. Reward his release of the toy with the food treat.
9. Give him lots of praise and pats.
10. Repeat steps 2 through 9 intermittently throughout the day or week before trying to make the exercise more difficult.

As you work with your Shih Tzu, you will be amazed at the things he will hold in his mouth for you on command. (This skill can make for some great photos.) When he becomes very reliable holding

(1) Offer your Shih Tzu something that you know he will take. As soon as he has it in his mouth, say "Take it!"

(2) Allow him to hold his prize for a few moments.

(3) Offer him a treat and say "Out" as he drops the prize.

(4) Give your Shih Tzu his reward!

items for you, introduce different materials. Instead of just soft, plush toys, ask him to hold a wooden dumbbell, a plastic water bottle, a ball, and the most disliked substance of all, something metal, such as a spoon (or small dumbbell).

The more items that you ask your Shih Tzu to hold, the more opportunities you'll have to ask him to release the item, using the *out* command. Even if you're not planning on competing in obedience, it's comforting to know that if your Shih Tzu should pick up something dangerous, you will be able to give him the *out* command and recover the item.

Leave It

Imagine you're out for a walk and your Shih Tzu spies a dead mouse in the gutter. The item is within reach of your dog and you can't reel in your leash quickly enough to keep him away from it.

If you've taught your Shih Tzu the *leave it* command, he should walk right by.

Teaching the *leave it* is something you can work on both in the home with items you've set out and when out on walks.

1. With your Shih Tzu on-leash, walk past the object you've planted. (Make sure the object is just slightly interesting; you don't want to use something your Shih Tzu would find virtually irresistible.)
2. Keep the leash short enough so he can't reach the object.
3. As he begins to veer toward the object, say "Leave it" and turn away from the object.
4. As your Shih Tzu turns to follow you, distract him with a squeaky toy.

5. Mark the correct behavior (leaving the object and moving toward you) with a click or "Yes!"
6. Reward the behavior with praise, pats, and a treat and/or play with the squeaky toy.
7. Release your Shih Tzu with "Okay" or a chest pat to let him know that he's finished with the exercise.
8. Repeat the exercise a few times—and then move onto something else.

When you go on walks with your Shih Tzu, keep an eye out for items that he might like to taste, pick up, or flop down and roll in. Use these opportunities to practice *leave it*.

Over time, you will say "Leave it," and your Shih Tzu will veer back to you. If you miss an object and your Shih Tzu picks up something he shouldn't, use the *out* command. If all else fails, keep a supply of treats on hand. In addition to sporadically working on various exercises, you can offer them as a swap.

The *leave it* command can help to get even a "stick loving" Shih Tzu to ignore twigs.

Home Schooling

Where to Train and When to Add Distractions

One of the best places to begin training a new skill to your Shih Tzu is in the privacy, security, and seclusion of your own home. The fewer distractions your puppy or adult has when learning a new behavior, the more easily your Shih Tzu can focus on understanding what you want him to do.

If your home is utter chaos—kids running through the kitchen, TVs blaring, and three other dogs practicing for their own circus—disregard the previous comment about your home being a training sanctuary. If your home is a zoo, you'll need to find a quiet place where you and your dog can work.

It's easier for a Shih Tzu to learn when there are few distractions.

Once your Shih Tzu is solid on an exercise, you can try a different location such as the backyard. With grass, trees, and birds flitting about, there's plenty for a Shih Tzu to want to investigate.

When you add distractions by changing a dog's training location, reduce the exercise you are working on to the original shaping stage, in which you used a food lure to create the desired behavior. This gives your Shih Tzu the greatest chance of succeeding.

Many owners move to a more distracting location and try to pick up right where they left off with their training. If your dog is solid with his *down* in the quiet of your family room, but is asked to *down* in the front yard as a pack of kids runs by, he almost certainly won't lie down. He'll be too distracted. However, he's not too distracted to remember that you gave him the *down* command and that he got away with not lying down. Now you've created a situation in which your dog believes he can hear the command *down* and not lie down. Some trainers estimate that it takes 20 correct repetitions to undo one distracted mistake.

Whenever you make an exercise more difficult by changing the location of your training session, make the exercise itself easier for the dog. You want him to succeed, you want to build confidence, and you want it to be fun. Building the exercise back up to your current working level may take more than one training session.

Adding Distractions

New locations will provide new distractions—particularly those you can't control—all on their own. If you'd like to make an exercise

more difficult for your dog by *adding* distractions, while in your home, you'll still need to make the exercise itself easier.

Let's say you're working on a *down-stay*. You're currently able to put your dog in a *down-stay*, stand 10 feet away, and have him hold the *down-stay* for at least five minutes. Now you want to have someone walk by with her dog. That's too *big* of a distraction.

Make it easier by putting your Shih Tzu in the *down-stay* and remaining by his side as the dog and handler walk by. From this level, gradually build on the exercise by increasing only one aspect of the exercise at a time. In other words, increase the time your Shih Tzu stays in a *down-stay* (time) or how many steps you take from your Shih Tzu while he's in the *down-stay* (distance), but never increase two factors at the same time.

Though it may take time to build up an exercise, if your Shih Tzu remains confident and happy throughout the process, you'll have an enthusiastic training companion who is *very* consistent and solid in his work.

10 *Correcting Annoying Behaviors*

Dogs don't come pre-wired to know what we humans find insanely annoying or just plain bothersome. Without instruction, dogs will naturally default to dog rules. Almost every "problem" behavior a puppy or adult dog owner encounters is usually quite acceptable behavior among dogs. Your job is to help show your Shih Tzu which behaviors are and aren't allowed and give him alternative ways to communicate what he needs or wants.

Barking

Shih Tzu bark for many different reasons. They are often fairly reliable "alert" dogs. (not guard dogs, watch dogs, or protection dogs). If a Shih Tzu hears something, he will sound the alert. If he finds the sound suspicious, he will continue barking the alarm. Having a reliable alert dog is a nice filter for those who live alone or who tend to jump at the slightest noise.

Barking also occurs for many other reasons. Your Shih Tzu may bark if you aren't paying enough attention to him; if you've let someone in the house that he's never met before; if his favorite toy has rolled

under the couch and he can't reach it; if he feels it is time for dinner; if he thinks he'd like a cookie; or if he wants you to play with him.

Though the breed is not generally known for being "barky," there are Shih Tzu who develop the habit. There are a couple of tactics you can take to combat this.

Ignore him. Dogs trained to alert the hearing impaired to important sounds (the doorbell, smoke alarm, oven timer, phone, etc.) are uncharacteristically quiet. They are trained to run back and forth between the source of the sound (except in the case of a smoke alarm) and the deaf owner, pawing at the person's legs to get her attention. The dogs usually don't bark because barking doesn't get them anything. The owner can't hear the sound, so it does the dogs no good to bark for attention, cookies, or scraps.

The theory behind ignoring a dog's barking in a hearing home is the same: if the incessant barking doesn't achieve anything positive for the dog, the dog will find another way to communicate what he wants. His barking may temporarily peak (a last-ditch effort to get people to pay attention to him) and then it will naturally subside. This method takes patience, consistency, and in some cases, a set of ear plugs.

There is an exception to the don't-respond-and-he'll-stop-barking rule. If the dog finds barking is self-rewarding, he'll keep at it. For example, when a delivery person rings the doorbell, leaves a package, and trots back to the truck, the dog truly believes his barking has driven the person away. In the Shih Tzu's mind, he has won! So, in cases such as this, ignoring a dog's barking isn't always the answer.

Make use of the *down* command. Another way to handle a Shih Tzu's barking—whether it's to chase away the delivery person or try to talk you out of a piece of toast on your plate—is to put the Shih Tzu in a *down-stay*. It's very difficult for dogs to bark when they are in a *down*. Once the dog is quiet, reward him for the *down*. Be sure he has been in the *down* long enough to know that you are rewarding the *down* and not his barking.

Exercise your Shih Tzu! Ever notice how dogs don't bark in their sleep? A tired, contented dog is a good dog in many, many ways. A bored dog, however, will be much more vocal. If you aren't taking your Shih Tzu out for at least two brisk, 20-minute walks each day, try adding this exercise into your daily routine. Also scatter little training and play sessions throughout the day to exercise your Shih Tzu both mentally and physically. If he's well exercised, mentally stimulated, and feels you are giving him lots of attention, you'll probably end up with a much quieter dog.

Remove or minimize your dog's barking triggers. If your dog enjoys barking

Shih Tzu bark for many reasons; however, if your dog barks excessively, the *speak* and *hush* commands can make for a quieter household.

at the delivery man and various neighbors, children, dogs, and other moving objects that pass by your home, don't allow him access to the front door. This type of barking is only self-rewarding if people, dogs, and things go away. If you keep your Shih Tzu gated and away from the front door, he won't be rewarded by being able to "drive off" these interlopers. He will still be a good alert dog, but with no perceived reward, the incessant barking should taper off.

Bark On Command

Why would anyone in their right mind want to teach a dog that already barks too much to bark? Easy. In teaching your Shih Tzu to bark on command, you are also teaching him to hush. Much like the

It's difficult for even the barkiest of Shih Tzu to make a noise while lying down.

take it and *out* commands, the two commands go hand in hand.

To teach *speak* and *hush*, you'll use free-shaping, or giving a command when the dog is already providing the behavior you want.

1. When your Shih Tzu stops barking and is being quiet, say "Hush."
2. Mark the behavior with a click or "Yes!"
3. Reward the behavior.
4. Repeat. Say "Hush" as often as you find your Shih Tzu stops barking to be quiet. Always mark and reward the behavior.
5. Now, ask for a bark from your Shih Tzu. Is there a certain playful way you can look at your Shih Tzu that will get him to bark? Will he bark if you have a treat in your hand or squeak a certain toy? Your goal is to get your Shih Tzu to produce a playful, fun bark. You do

not want to make him bark because he is stressed or nervous.

6. While he is barking, give the command "Speak!"
7. Mark the behavior with a click or "Yes!"
8. Reward the behavior with a treat, praise, and attention.
9. When your Shih Tzu is quiet for several long seconds, say "Hush."
10. Mark the behavior.
11. Reward the behavior with more treats, praise, and attention.
12. Repeat as often as you can until your Shih Tzu begins associating speak with active barking and hush with being quiet. Your goal is to be able to say "Hush" when you don't want your Shih Tzu barking, and to give your fun-loving Shih Tzu plenty of opportunities to bark when you say "Speak."

Bolting

Some folks will tell you that a dog that likes to push his way past you to bolt out the front door is "dominant" and possibly on the way to being "trouble." With the Shih Tzu, this is highly unlikely. Pushing past owners in doorways, particularly to bolt out the front door, is generally the sign of an excited puppy or dog that hasn't learned all the rules yet and is most likely in need of more exercise and "out" time.

Of course, whether your Shih Tzu bolts out the front door every time you crack it open because he wants a car ride, a walk, or to take a wild and crazy run around the front yard, it's a dangerous practice. Most people live near roads and where there are roads there are cars and drivers who aren't looking. Even if drivers are looking, a little flash of hair making a dash for the street may not catch a person's eye until it's too late.

To keep your puppy or dog safe and sound, get bolting under control.

Take your Shih Tzu out frequently. The more walks, car rides, and playtime your Shih Tzu gets, the less likely he is to feel the need to make a bolt for freedom. Additionally, if your Shih Tzu gets lots of exercise and mental stimulation outdoors, he'll be pleasantly tired and more relaxed when in the home.

Consider gating your porch or fencing your front yard. Think of this as a holding area for your Shih Tzu. A house with a front, railed porch can easily have a gate added to the entryway, allowing your Shih Tzu a great, shaded, breezy place to hang outside when you're working in the yard

Chasing a squirrel is very rewarding for this Shih Tzu, and encourages barking.

or spending time on your porch. If you don't have a porch, can you fence in a small area of your front yard? Many neighborhoods allow picketed front yards. Either of these options provide an area to hold your Shih Tzu.

Limit front door access. If you can't control the outside environment restrict your Shih Tzu's access to the front door. There are many types of dog gates available on the market. Pressure-type gates can be set up anywhere, and can be purchased with a swinging gate insert that makes it easy for you to walk through.

Another way to keep your escape artist from wriggling out is to put him in an exercise pen or crate every time you answer the door. As soon as you've shut the door, he can come right back out.

Teach the *sit-stay*. As a general rule, it's good practice to teach your Shih Tzu to sit and wait while you go through doorways. This helps to establish gentle leadership and it keeps your Shih Tzu from getting underfoot as you both try to go through the open door. Teaching the *sit-stay* at the front door is helpful for another reason: it's a good command to teach at the top of the front porch or stoop so you can go down the steps without getting pulled by an enthusiastic dog. Once at the bottom of the steps, you can release your Shih Tzu from the *sit-stay* to come and join you.

To prevent bolting, snap a leash on your Shih Tzu and put him in a *sit-stay* (see page 86) a couple of feet from the front door. At first don't open the door at all. When he's reliably holding a *sit-stay* in front of the door for several minutes, take a step (with your right foot) to the door and step back. Mark, reward, release.

Next you'll want to work toward taking a step to the door, holding the handle, and stepping back. See where this is going? Once you can step all the way to the door, give the *sit-stay* command, walk to the door, turn the door knob, and return to your dog. Keep working until you can step forward, turn the knob, open the door a few inches, keep it there for a few minutes, and then shut the door.

Your goal is to work up to being able to put your Shih Tzu in a *sit-stay*, open the front door, walk two steps out onto the stoop, hold the door open, stand a few minutes with the door open, and then return back inside. If you are working with a six-foot leash, you should have plenty of length to accomplish this (your Shih Tzu should be one to two feet from the front door). If you'd like to work with a longer leash, purchase a recall line or snap a second leash to the grip loop of the first leash.

Meanwhile, until you've gotten your Shih Tzu to the point where you can open and shut the door (while he's on-leash and in a *sit-stay*), don't allow him access to the door when you answer it. Put him in his crate or behind a gate. An accidental escape will set your door training back a few steps.

Work on Recall. Obviously, practicing a dog's recall doesn't change the Shih Tzu's bolting habits; however, if he gets out the door, knowing that he will come when you call him significantly lessens the chance that your puppy or adult will get lost or seriously injured. The *come* should always be practiced on a line, so that the Shih Tzu can't fail. Your hope is that if you have to use it in a real situation, your Shih Tzu will indeed come to you, since that's what he's always done before.

Reinforce the *sit* at a distance. This is another emergency back-up plan, not a solution to bolting. Often a dog won't respond to *come*; however, most dogs will *sit*. If you practice the *sit* frequently, try adding some distance to the command. Then, when your Shih Tzu bolts out the

---

TZU TIP

Prior to working on the sit-stay at the front door, take your Shih Tzu for a nice walk. It can be borderline cruel to work on training your Shih Tzu not to bolt if he hasn't already been outside for sufficient physical and mental stimulation.

Jumping up is a friendly behavior that can be easily controlled by teaching the *sit* command.

door, say "Sit!" This may give you the few moments you need to go over to scoop him up.

Remember, when you do recapture your Shih Tzu, do not punish him. The act of bolting is long past. Reward him for a good *sit* and take him inside. Resolve to work on the *sit-stay* at the door, exercise him more, and try to create a front door situation that's more controllable.

Jumping Up

Shih Tzu are adorable when they want your attention. It comes quite naturally to them to dance on their hind legs and bat their front paws in the air. They also enjoy getting pats and being picked up, so if they feel you're ignoring them, they may start jumping up on you and pawing at your legs.

If you've got a puppy, you probably react to this by scooping the puppy up and cuddling him. They're hard to resist! But, picking up a puppy every time he jumps up on you teaches him to jump up.

If you've adopted an adult dog, you may find that your Shih Tzu already tends to "jump up" for everything: attention, treats, greeting new people in the home, or to be picked up.

This is not a big problem and can usually be handled quite easily. If you've got a Shih Tzu who likes to jump for joy, your biggest concern will be curbing the jumping without squashing her enthusiasm. Jumping up is a friendly greeting that needs to be tempered gently.

Work on *sit-stay*. If your Shih Tzu is in a *sit*, he isn't jumping up. Reward him for his *sit-stay* with lots of hands-on praise and pats. When he learns that he gets more attention in the *sit*, he'll actually get to the point where you won't have to tell him to *sit*, he'll do it automatically.

Teach the *hup*! Counterintuitive, yes, but teaching a dog to jump up on command (along with a solid *sit-stay*) can help keep him from jumping up when he's not supposed to.

1. With your Shih Tzu on leash, put him in a *sit-stay*.
2. Take a treat in one hand, look him in the eye playfully, and begin to crouch a little.

113

3. Just before he breaks the *sit-stay*, and with the treat only an inch from his nose, quickly say, "Hup!"
4. Encourage him to stretch for the treat.
5. Mark the behavior with a click or "yes!"
6. Reward him with praise and pats (he's already got the treat).
7. Repeat steps 1 through 6. As he figures out that it's okay to break the *sit* to jump for the treat, begin moving the treat a little farther away from his nose. Eventually, you'll have it a couple of feet from his nose and he'll be hopping up like a circus dog on command.

Practice this exercise on good footing only. Slick floors could result in an injury. Also, do not ask your Shih Tzu to jump more than two feet from the ground. If your Shih Tzu has joint disease or other musculoskeletal problems, don't attempt this exercise with him at all.

Nipping

Puppies and young adults of all breeds can be quite mouthy. Dogs by nature are quite "oral"—they investigate, play, solve problems, move, and pull items with their mouths.

Additionally, teething puppies have a real need to chew and gnaw on things and with a new set of adult teeth, adolescent dogs enjoy chewing on a good bone.

The problem occurs when the Shih Tzu attempts to chew on you or a family member. If a puppy has spent a lot of time with his littermates and mom, he will usually have good bite inhibition—he knows how hard is too hard. What he often doesn't

(1) Put your Shih Tzu in a *sit*, holding a treat close to his nose.
(2) Encourage him to reach and jump for the treat, saying "Hup!" when he jumps up.
(3) Reward him!

know is that it's not okay to nip and bite the human members of the family.

These tactics will get your Shih Tzu to stop nipping.

1. **Give him something else to do.** Puppies and young Shih Tzu nip when they're tremendously excited. Nipping often occurs right as you walk in the front door. To solve this, keep a few favorite toys at the front door. As you step in the door, give the *take it* command. With a toy in his mouth, he can't nip you.

2. **Let him know it hurts!** Nipping is not a behavior to ignore. (He'll just learn to nip harder next time.) When he chomps on you, say "Ow!" loudly, turn your back on him, and absolutely refuse to give him any attention for several minutes.

3. **Practice calming exercises.** Since nipping is usually the result of too much excitement, recognize when your Shih Tzu is about to nip and try to quietly settle him before he crosses that line.

4. **Work on *sit-stay* and/or *down-stay*.** These exercises will help to calm your Shih Tzu and distract him from nipping you.

5. **Set rules with children.** If you have kids, always supervise them when they are with your Shih Tzu. Children don't always behave appropriately with puppies and dogs. They can get pretty wild and this is just the excuse your Shih Tzu needs to get wild too.

Begging

Your Shih Tzu can smell your food. He's convinced it's better than his dinner. He wants a taste, so he looks at you and dances in a little circle. You're still not giving in so he starts barking, then pawing at your leg.

Begging, no matter what the size of the dog, is annoying. Fortunately, there are ways to prevent and stop this behavior.

1. **Never feed from the table.** If you feed your Shih Tzu scraps from the table, you are setting him up to beg. If you want to feed your Shih Tzu a few scraps, carry your plate back to the kitchen, give the *sit* command, and reward him with the treat.

2. **Ignore him.** Don't make eye contact, pet him, scold, or talk to your Shih Tzu. Begging behaviors will initially escalate (they worked before, so for a period of days he may try even harder to get your attention), but eventually they will subside.

3. **Watch for enablers.** Do you have a significant other or child who is giving your Shih Tzu scraps from the table when you aren't looking? Unless you can get everyone to ignore your Shih Tzu, he will continue to beg.

4. **Practice the *down-stay* during meals.** Initially, it's going to take a lot of work to get your Shih Tzu to lie down on his bed while you eat dinner. A good *down-stay* is well worth the work to have a little peace at meals.

5. **Crate him with something yummy.** Put your Shih Tzu's crate in the room where you eat (so he can see you) and give him a favorite chew bone. Make it particularly yummy by smearing a little peanut butter on one end.

11 *Training for Travel*

One of the greatest benefits of owning a Shih Tzu is that you can take your puppy or dog with you almost anywhere. The breed is small, so he can be carried in an over-the-shoulder soft carrier or pushed along in a doggie stroller. Shih Tzu fit in airline-approved, "in-cabin" carriers, so they are welcome on many flights (with reservations). Shih Tzu on-leash or in carriers can travel on many types of public transportation in most big cities.

The Portable Shih Tzu

As well-suited as the Shih Tzu is for traveling both across town and cross country, carting him around is only enjoyable if he travels well. The biggest mistake many pet owners make is springing a big trip on their puppies or dogs with no prior practice.

Without practice, the Shih Tzu won't be used to a carrier, or acclimated to the movement of the car or plane. He'll likely get sick to his stomach or be so nervous that his bowels are on overdrive. An accident with a coated breed is an awful mess, particularly when you don't have ready access to a sink or bathtub to clean him.

Fortunately, even the most nervous canine traveler can be calmed over time with patience and a lot of practice. If you are planning a trip that will involve significant time in a car, plane, boat, or other form of transportation, and you own a Shih Tzu that is a bit anxious about travel in general, try to start conditioning him for the trip at least four to six weeks in advance.

Acclimation to the Carrier

Your first and most important step in developing a good canine traveler is acclimating him to his crate. Your Shih Tzu needs to feel that his carrier is a safe and comfy place to lie while the rest of the world is moving.

To help your Shih Tzu not only accept his crate, but learn to enjoy spending time in it, try the following:

1. **Place the carrier in a busy place.** Wherever you're going to be, put the carrier in that room on the floor with the door open. You want your Shih Tzu to get used to its presence and feel comfortable walking in and out of it

but you don't want your Shih Tzu to associate the crate with punishment, which he might do if he is kept in an isolated location.

2. **Make it super comfy.** Put comfortable bedding in the carrier so that your Shih Tzu will want to curl up in it for naps. If he has a favorite snuggly bed or blanket, put it in the crate. It should be something soft and familiar to him.

3. **Feed him in the carrier.** If your Shih Tzu eats all of his meals in the carrier, he will begin to associate good things with the crate.

4. **Provide treats and chew toys.** Again, the more wonderful things that are associated with the carrier, the more willing your Shih Tzu will be to ride in it.

Most Shih Tzu will be happily gnawing on their bones in a closed carrier before the week is finished. If, however, he's had a bad experience in a crate or carrier, he may be so stressed with the crate that none of the above is enough to tempt him to even enter.

If this is the case for your Shih Tzu, don't try to force the issue. Continue to help him through his fears and build up more good experiences than bad.

1. **Spray D.A.P. lightly on the interior of the carrier.** This chemical is harmless to dogs and mimics the comforting pheromone that is emitted by nursing females. Puppies and adults recognize it and studies show that it can have a calming effect.

2. **Toss treats into the carrier.** If your Shih Tzu is reluctant to eat his meals in the crate (i.e., he'd rather starve than

A travel-savvy Shih Tzu can accompany you to some amazing places.

go in there), sit by the carrier and make a little trail of treats up to and just inside the open door. Don't make a big deal about it but do praise him when he reaches in and takes the final treat. Work on tossing the treat farther and farther back into the crate. It's fine if he goes in, retrieves the treat, and eats it elsewhere. At least he's venturing into the carrier.

3. **Remove the roof.** Your Shih Tzu may dislike feeling closed in. Remove the top half of a plastic carrier and it becomes very bedlike when a plush pillow is placed in the bottom half. As your Shih Tzu begins using the "bed," you can reintroduce the top half.

117

Acclimating to the carrier is an important first step to raising a traveling Shih Tzu.

rest in the crate on his own, encourage him to enter it by tossing a treat into the crate. Toss the treat far enough back into the crate that he has to get his entire body inside.

2. Once he's inside, give your command.
3. Mark the behavior with a click or "Yes!"
4. Reward the behavior with praise and a treat.
5. Release him from the crate by saying, "Okay!" When he comes out of the crate, give him lots of pats and praise.
6. Repeat steps 1 through 4 several times a day. Before long all you will need to do is have a treat in your hand and sit or kneel by the carrier to have your Shih Tzu hop right in—possibly even before you give the command.

Teaching In *or* Go to Your Crate

Now that you've got your Shih Tzu comfortable with visiting his crate and coming back out, you'll want to be able to add a command for him to enter the crate. "In," "Go to your crate," and "Kennel up," are several commands that work well, but you can choose any words you'd like.

Teaching this command relies mostly on free-shaping to associate the word with the behavior.

1. If your Shih Tzu is in the carrier, sit or kneel next to it and say, "Go to your crate." If your Shih Tzu doesn't sleep or

Teaching Wait

After a puppy or dog has been in a crate for a little while, he is often impatient to get out. He may have an urgent need to relieve himself, he may have missed you something awful, or he may just want out of the carrier.

The *wait* command comes in handy at times like these, particularly when you need your Shih Tzu to stand still for a minute as you reach in to snap a leash on him. A Shih Tzu that acts like a greased pig coming out of a starting gate is very dangerous to travel with—he can get loose and lost very easily.

So, if you crack the door to your pup's carrier and he tries to bolt out, this command is for you.

1. Put your Shih Tzu in his carrier and shut the door.

When traveling by car, it is not a bad idea to bring along an exercise pen for safe containment once at your destination.

2. Raise your hand to the carrier door, palm toward your Shih Tzu, and say, "Wait."
3. Mark the behavior with a click or "Yes."
4. Reward the behavior with praise.
5. Release him from the exercise by saying "Okay!" and completely opening the door.
6. Repeat steps 1 through 5.
7. After ten or more successful repetitions, put your Shih Tzu in his carrier, shut the door and then barely crack it open, while saying "Wait." Mark, reward, release.

Your goal is to have your Shih Tzu associate *wait* with staying in the carrier as the door is opened progressively wider. Ultimately, you want to be able to say "Wait," swing the door to the carrier completely open, reach in, clip a leash to your dog's collar, and then say "Okay," allowing him to bounce out of his crate.

Train in small steps, with no distractions and in the safety of your home. (If he does bolt out, there's no danger.) Then, as he gets more proficient, practice in the car in the garage. By the time you take your Shih Tzu to the dog park (where he'll be very excited about getting out of his crate as quickly as possible), he'll be very solid on his wait command.

Introducing the Car

If your Shih Tzu had a traumatic "first trip home," consider breaking down his next car introduction into smaller components: the car, the seat where he will ride, the closing of the doors, and finally, turning on the engine. Feel free to jump to the next step without multiple repetitions if your Shih Tzu is completely comfortable with the current step.

1. **Place the crate next to the car.** Let your Shih Tzu see what you are doing. Open and shut the car doors, keeping an eye on his response. Speak casually to him. Pick up the crate with him in it and take him back into the house. Release him and give him a little play time as a reward. Repeat as necessary until he is comfortable with sitting in the crate next to the car.

2. **Place the crate in the car, keeping the doors open.** Sit next to your Shih Tzu and discuss the latest news, where you're thinking of going on vacation next, or what really bothers you about the neighbors next door. Reach over and

Plan fun destinations so your Shih Tzu will look forward to car rides.

strap the carrier into the seat belt. Undo the seat belt, pick up the carrier, set him down outside the car, shut up the car and carry the carrier and dog back into the house. Release and reward him.

3. **Feed your Shih Tzu in the crate, in the car.** If you are getting tired of carrying a crate in and out of the house and you don't mind buying a second carrier, put one in your car permanently. Bring your Shih Tzu out at mealtimes to eat in his car carrier. Sit with him while he's eating and then take him back inside. Good boy!

4. **Put the crate in the car, shut the doors, and sit in the driver's seat.** Since most cars have airbags in the front passenger's side, it's not safe to strap a dog carrier in this seat. He'll have to sit in his carrier in back, so it's a good idea to get him used to being one row of seats away from you.

5. **Start the car.** Let it run for a few minutes. Turn the car off.

6. **Add movement. Start the car and roll down the driveway.** If all is going well take a short drive around the block and return to the driveway. Cut the engine, take your Shih Tzu inside, release him from the carrier, and make a big deal over him.

Building up for the First Road Trip

If your Shih Tzu is comfortable with his crate or carrier and completely at home sitting in the car, it's time to get moving! You'll want to keep these first few rides very, very brief and build slowly. Watch for signs of stress in your Shih Tzu and try to end the car ride before he shows signs of anxiety.

Additionally, plan your drives so that after five or ten minutes you can take a break, get your Shih Tzu out of the car (this will help if he's beginning to feel queasy), and take a walk with him or play an on-leash game with a toy.

Find a park that's close by and spend at least an equal amount of time playing there. No parks in the area? Go to a nearby, dog-friendly subdivision where you can walk your Shih Tzu for several minutes.

Preparing for a Calm Drive

There are many steps you can take to help your Shih Tzu relax while in the car.

1. **Have your dog relieve himself prior to getting in the car.** The potty command works well for this.
2. **Exercise your Shih Tzu.** Take him for a walk or play a game of fetch. Let him burn off a little energy so he's not as anxious and is even a little tired or sleepy.
3. **Keep it short.** Build up from going around the block to driving around the neighborhood to going out for a longer trip. Watch for signs of anxiety and try

Training a Shih Tzu to lie on a blanket, no matter where you place it, comes in handy when traveling or when visiting another person's home.

to time things, so that your Shih Tzu doesn't start showing signs of stress of car sickness.

4. **Don't coddle him.** If your Shih Tzu starts crying, whining, or barking, don't sympathize with him ("Oh, you poor baby!"). Instead, speak conversationally and with confidence. ("You're doing a great job, boy. We'll be at the park in a minute and that is going to be so much fun.") Also, make a note to yourself when the stress symptoms began to appear and try to make your ride slightly shorter the next time.

121

5. **Stay calm.** Some behaviorists who work with dogs suffering from car sickness feel that the calmness and confidence of the owner has a lot to do with how the puppy or dog reacts to the car. If you are a nervous driver, your Shih Tzu could be picking up on that. Try to work on your own calming techniques. And for you road-rage types, refrain from loud outbursts and fist shaking. Your Shih Tzu will think this is being directed at him (or that his owner really has gone nuts).

6. **Don't over stimulate him.** Bombarding a Shih Tzu that's trying to acclimate to car travel with the radio cranked to your favorite song is not going to help. It will overwhelm him. What you might try, however, is playing a CD (at low volume) of canine calming music.

7. **Keep it cool.** Make sure that your Shih Tzu is getting plenty of fresh, cool air. If he's on a side that's getting sun, he could be quite hot even if you're cool. If the rear seating area doesn't receive much air, consider attaching a battery operated fan to your dog's crate.

8. **Listen for pleas to relieve himself.** The motion and excitement of travel can increase a puppy's or dog's metabolism to the point that he will need to eliminate much faster than if he were lounging around the house. If he's asking to "go," pull over to a safe location and allow him to relieve himself.

9. **Bring cleaning supplies.** Extra bedding, paper towels, water bottles, baby powder (to sprinkle on wet "ick" so that it can be brushed out of the Shih Tzu coat, allowing him to be more comfortable for the ride back), and a clean towel are essential.

Other Travel Skills

With your Shih Tzu acclimated to the crate and travel in the car, you're ready to go for short trips. To help make longer, multiple day excursions easy, consider working on a few more travel skills.

Elimination on command. The *go potty* command will help make it easier for you to get your Shih Tzu to relieve himself in unfamiliar places and on strange surfaces.

Pee pad training. If you frequently travel with your Shih Tzu, or if you plan on flying with him, he may have an urgent need when you find yourself in an airport or subway station. If you can go into a bathroom stall and lay down a pee pad for your Shih Tzu—and he'll use it—life will be a lot easier.

***Go to Your Place* command.** You're tired. You're settling into your hotel room, but your Shih Tzu can't seem to find a place to curl up on the bed. He's stressed. You're stressed. It's going to be a long night.

TZU TIP

When traveling, freeze the water in the bottle (leave a little room for expansion) and secure it to the door of your Shih Tzu's crate. He'll be able to take little sips to keep from becoming dehydrated, but he won't drink so much in one setting that you'll have to stop 20 minutes after he's lapped up a bowl of water.

Before you get yourself in this situation, train your Shih Tzu to lie on a small blanket, wherever you put it. Then, when you travel, you can simply take his blanket and lay it where you'd like him to sleep on the bed.

1. Lay the blanket of your choice on the floor.
2. While on-leash, walk your Shih Tzu over to the blanket.
3. When all four paws are on the blanket, say, "Go to your place."
4. Mark with a click or "Yes!"
5. Reward with praise and a treat.
6. Release by saying, "Okay!" and/or with a pat on the chest.
7. Walk him off the blanket and repeat the exercise.
8. As he gets the idea, begin to give the command as he is putting his back two paws onto the blanket, then as he is putting his front paws on the blanket. Make sure all four paws are on the blanket before you mark the behavior with the click or "Yes!"

Your goal is to be able to say, "Go to your place," and have your Shih Tzu start looking for his blanket. Make sure that your Shih Tzu understands that *place* is a spot where he can relax.

As your Shih Tzu starts associating *place* with being on the blanket, put the blanket in different locations. If he has a favorite place to snuggle on the couch, put the blanket there. (You can do some free-shaping, too. If he goes to the blanket to curl up, take advantage of this opportunity and say, "Go to your place.")

When you're in your hotel room, or at a park or eating outdoors in a café, you can lay your Shih Tzu's blanket beside you,

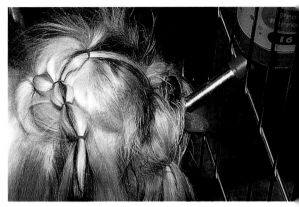

Training your Shih Tzu to drink from a water bottle will help keep his travel carrier dry.

tell him to "Go to your place," and presto! He will! And, he'll know that he can relax and even take a snooze, if he'd like.

New drinking skills. Teaching your Shih Tzu to use a pet drinking bottle can be very helpful while traveling. You won't have to worry about spills from a bowl. You also won't have to physically stop the car so that you can offer your Shih Tzu water. (If he's in a full coat, drinking from a water bottle keeps the coat under his chin from getting soaked and stained, too.)

Usually, all you have to do is fill the water bottle and fasten it so that the metal tube extends at a comfortable height for your Shih Tzu to reach while standing. If he shows no interest in checking out how the contraption works, try putting the tiniest bit of honey or even an ultra-thin smear of peanut butter on the end of the nozzle. When your Shih Tzu licks the nozzle, water will drip into his mouth. To help him further make the connection, pick up his normal water bowl and make the water bottle available to him 24/7.

Offer a "busy" bone. For many puppies and dogs, the action of gnawing on a bone or chew toy is very calming and comforting. Think of it as a canine pacifier. Figure out what your Shih Tzu likes to chew on the most, make sure it's safe and doesn't break into sharp pieces or sections that could be swallowed or choked on, and provide this for gnawing on during your travels.

Overcoming Car Sickness

Most cases of car sickness—excessive panting, drooling, vomiting, mobile bowels, etc.—are stress induced. Once the source of the dog's stress has been addressed and he's become comfortable with his carrier and the movement of the car, the dog's episodes of car sickness dissipate and eventually disappear.

There are, however, a few dogs that continue to suffer. If you have been working and working with your Shih Tzu and he just can't seem to get over his car sick-

---

TZU TIP

Puppies often go through a period of motion sickness. Some believe this has something to do with the development of the inner ear or ear canal. Whatever the reason, most puppies outgrow this and have no problems with motion sickness as an adult.

---

ness, schedule an exam with your veterinarian. He or she may find the crux of the problem and can offer assistance.

If nothing unusual shows up on the exam, talk to your veterinarian about other ways you can help manage your Shih Tzu's motion sickness. Ginger snaps or a small piece of peppermint or licorice may have stomach calming effects. You also might try applying a drop of peppermint oil on the side of your pup's carrier.

Additionally, in January 2007 the Food and Drug Administration (FDA) approved the first medication (Cerenia) for treating canines with motion sickness. This medication may be of benefit to your Shih Tzu.

If all of these methods aren't helpful, consider leaving your Shih Tzu at home with a pet sitter or finding an excellent boarding kennel to take him when you're traveling. If he's miserable, he's not enjoying the trip.

Strategies for Airline Travel

In order to travel by air, your Shih Tzu will need to be acclimated to his crate and comfortable with the motion of a car. Flying is much smoother than car travel and seems to cause fewer problems with motion sickness, but if your Shih Tzu isn't comfortable with his carrier, he won't be happy.

Assuming he's fine with his carrier and travel, you'll want to make sure that your Shih Tzu is trained to use pee pads when necessary.

Teaching him to drink from a pet water bottle is also helpful because you won't be able to take him out of his carrier in the terminal or on the flight.

In addition to making sure you have all the appropriate paperwork, health documentation, and your Shih Tzu's ticket ready for your flight (information as to what is required by each carrier is available from the individual airline), teach your Shih Tzu to turn around in his carrier on command.

The ticket agent may ask you to prove that your Shih Tzu fits the crate. That means he's got to be able to turn completely around in the carrier. If your Shih Tzu decides at that moment not to comply, theoretically, the ticket agent could tell you that carrier is too small and your dog won't be allowed to fly in it.

Teaching the Turnaround

1. With your dog standing on the floor (he's not in his carrier at this point), show him a treat, and with your hand flat and palm down, lure him in a comfortable circle. (Not so big that he loses interest; not so tight that it's too difficult and he simply backs up.) Notice that your hand is making a visual signal of a circle. This is important for later!

   If he isn't comfortable going in the direction you've chosen, try the other direction. Dogs can favor one side (just

as we humans are right- or left-handed) and the opposite direction may be much easier for him.

2. As he circles, say "Turnaround!"
3. Mark the behavior with a click or "Yes!"
4. Reward him with the treat and lots of pats.
5. Release him with an "Okay!" and a quick pat on the chest.
6. Repeat the exercise, working to make the circle smaller and smaller, until he can easily and quickly whip around in place.
7. Put him in the carrier with the top unzipped.
8. Using the treat, repeat steps 1 through 7.
9. If you'd like, you can begin weaning the voice command from the exercise. If you use the *turnaround* in an actual airport, make sure you've got your Shih Tzu's attention before you attempt the trick sans voice.

Home Schooling

Manners for Public Transportation

Small dogs are able to travel with their owners in many large cities, using a variety of public transportation forms. Buses, trains, subways, ferries, and streetcars are frequently open to pet owners and their dogs. Perhaps the most important aspect of using public transportation is knowing what you can and can't do.

The most common restrictions for public transportation are:

■ The dog must be small (under 20 pounds)
■ The dog must be in a carrier
■ The dog must have proof of vaccinations (this can be kept in the carrier)

■ A pass or reduced rate ticket must be purchased for the dog
■ Passage is restricted to low-traffic, non-commuting hours
■ Passage is restricted to weekends or certain days

To find out which restrictions apply to pet owners for a specific city's transportation, check with the city's Department of Transportation.

Pet Etiquette

If you are allowed to travel with your Shih Tzu on a bus, ferry, or subway, don't interpret this to mean that you are *entitled* to travel on the bus, ferry, or subway with your dog. If, while you are riding, there is any inkling of a confrontation or "issue" with a non-pet-toting traveler, you will be the person asked to leave. Be forewarned!

In the Bag

In order to travel safely and without confrontation (yes, there are people who really don't like dogs in this world), the best approach is to keep your Shih Tzu as inconspicuous as possible. Choose your travel carrier carefully as you will be up close and personal with hundreds of strangers. You'll want a carrier that is comfortable for your Shih Tzu, but doesn't shout, "I am a dog carrier."

Choose a travel carrier that looks more like a stylish, large purse. Or, if you are a man (and a man bag is not your thing), consider purchasing a backpack made specifically for carrying dogs. (Sherpa makes a dark backpack that mimics those of college students.) Some carriers resemble a gym bag.

Keep Your Shih Tzu Contained

In addition to traveling with a carrier that doesn't look like a carrier, don't be tempted to let your cute little Shih Tzu poke his head out for kisses. This is a big no-no. First, if you haven't worked on your *wait* command, he may come flying out of the carrier. A loose dog is a lost dog! Don't risk this.

Second, it's virtually a guarantee that if you bend a rule by letting him poke his head out of the carrier, someone is going to complain. If, however, you've kept your pup under wraps and no one is aware that he's even there, then you shouldn't have any complaints.

Though this is a cute, hands-free way to carry a Shih Tzu, it would not be an acceptable way to travel on public transportation with your pet.

Keep Clean

Shih Tzu can develop a slight, unappealing oily odor to their skin if they aren't groomed frequently. Make sure that when you're traveling in tight quarters your Shih Tzu is clean and smells nice and his carrier is spotless and odorless, too.

Keep Quiet

Barking, whining, and yelping are all dead giveaways that you are carrying a pooch (and provide an opportunity for a non-dog lover to complain). To keep your Shih Tzu quiet, prepare him for travel. Make sure he's acclimated to his carrier and the movement of the vehicle. Also, ensure that he's had sufficient potty breaks that sudden urges won't be a problem.

And finally, if you know your Shih Tzu likes to talk a bit, work on the *hush* and *speak* commands before you travel on a crowded mode of public transportation.

When traveling on public transportation, it's important for pet owners to be more polite and conscientious than everyone else. Don't try to bend the rules or behave as if you're a rock star. Your goal is to get from Point A to Point B as uneventfully as possible. If no one realizes you've got a pooch onboard, you've done well!

12 *Fun Activities with Your Shih Tzu*

A Shih Tzu is quite content to be the center of a family's attention and be the perfect, well-mannered house pet—if you teach him the rules. Of course, the Shih Tzu can be much more than a beloved companion; he can also be an athlete, a therapist, a model, and a canine competitor! There are so many activities, sports, and events that dogs can take part in these days that the hardest part may be in deciding what to try next.

Agility can be an excellent activity to help build a timid dog's confidence.

Agility

Agility is the fastest growing dog sport in the country. Much of this has to do with it being so much fun for the dog and the owner. Some of today's top competitors in the sport never intended to compete; often, they started taking classes just to have fun with their dogs, to find an outlet for a dog's energy, or to boost a fearful dog's confidence. They ended up staying because it was such a blast.

No matter what your dog's temperament, age, athletic abilities, or ability to learn, agility appeals to virtually everyone and every dog. At its most basic level, agility is the best fun you'll ever have with your Shih Tzu on a playground made for dogs. Teeter-totters, tunnels, A-frames, tire jumps, pole jumps, ramps, and chutes— how can it get any better?

There are currently six national organizations that award agility titles; within each organization, there are a wide variety of classes. Generally, the classes are divided by the height and again by the experience of the dog. Small dogs compete with small dogs and newbies to the sport never compete with seasoned veterans.

Though the way each organization runs its events is slightly different, the basic concept is that the dog and handler must complete a course of obstacles as quickly and with as few faults (mistakes) as possible. The handler may use only her voice and hand signals to direct the dog through the course.

Getting Started

- ■ **Get a complete health exam.** Shih Tzu can suffer from luxating patellas, bad hips, and dysplastic elbows—to name a few maladies. Make sure you aren't exacerbating any musculoskeletal conditions by getting a clean bill of health from your veterinarian.
- ■ **Know your dog's limits.** A minor health problem doesn't rule out agility, it just means you need to be a little more careful. For the dog with physical limits, you must take it slowly and know how to keep your dog comfortable.
- ■ **Find an agility club.** Theoretically, you could build your own agility course in

Agility can be enjoyed at a competitive level or practiced just for fun.

your backyard using online instructions. Or you could purchase agility practice equipment online. However, it's easier and less expensive to start with a course that's already built and maintained by a local agility club.

- ■ **Take classes.** Agility is taught using positive, reward-based training; however, learning how to signal your dog to go under, over, or through an obstacle takes a bit of finesse and is more easily learned from an experienced trainer who has "been-there-done-that." A training club specializing in agility will offer classes for novices to advanced competitors.

A potential agility Shih Tzu is a puppy or dog that

- ■ has a good energy level
- ■ is very attentive

> ### TZU TIP
> If you'd like to participate in AKC-sponsored events (agility, rally, obedience, tracking, etc.), your Shih Tzu must be either registered with the AKC or hold a Purebred Alternative Listing (PAL) number. (This was formerly known as an Indefinite Listing Privilege or ILP.) To receive a PAL number, you will need to fill out an application (downloadable from www.akc.org), send in two recent color photos of your Shih Tzu (a front view and a side view while standing), proof of spay/neuter, and a nominal application fee.

- stays focused
- is eager to learn and doesn't bore easily
- loves working for food or a toy
- is athletic

One of the best aspects of agility is that virtually every Shih Tzu can participate in agility and will gain a lot from the experience. Participation in the sport, whether at the highest echelons or just going to classes because it's fun and something different, is almost always a positive experience for handler and dog. Unregistered Shih Tzu and mixes are welcome in many organizations' events.

Animal-Assisted Therapy

The Shih Tzu is a very popular choice for therapy dog work. The breed is small, so he can easily be lifted to rest in a lap, lie on a bed, or sit on a table or bed tray, giving many more people access to touching and interacting with the dog.

The Shih Tzu also has an amazing coat. Whether kept in a full coat or clipped into a shorter style, petting the Shih Tzu is a wonderful tactile experience. And then there's the Shih Tzu's tremendous temperament. His "know no strangers" outlook on life makes this breed the superstar of therapy dogs.

Types of Therapy Work

Animal-assisted therapy (AAT) is much more than just pet visitation. You can find AAT dogs working at rehabilitation facilities, post-operative care units, palliative care, and hospice. Some AAT dogs work with children to help them relax as they go under anesthesia and are then in the recovery area to provide companionship when the child wakes up.

AAT dogs and handlers can get involved in other ways, too. An increasingly popular program is R.E.A.D, in which dogs are trained to carefully "listen" to a child's reading, periodically "pointing" to a word in the book for the child to "explain" to them. Other AAT dogs and handlers volunteer at shelters, schools for the disabled, residential treatment facilities for abused children, and programs for those with eating disorders.

The two largest, national certifying organizations for AAT are the Delta Society and Therapy Dog International. Certification requirements vary for these organizations, as well as regional and local groups; however, usually a handler and her dog

Few people can resist touching and interacting with a friendly Shih Tzu, making this breed one of the best for therapy dog work.

are required to have a Canine Good Citizen (CGC) certificate (see below), complete an AAT training class, and pass an AAT interview and skills/training test.

Certification testing for AAT/AFT work usually includes testing the dog's ability to handle a variety of different scenarios that mimic real, working therapy situations, such as a dropped metal tray, a rolling wheelchair, a sudden outburst, or a person approaching the dog with irregular movements. In addition, you should

- **Know your commands.** A little obedience goes a long way. Your Shih Tzu doesn't have to be an obedience whiz, but he should know *sit*, *stay*, *down*, and *come* well. He should also walk calmly on a leash.
- **Socialize with everyone.** The AAT Shih Tzu needs to be comfortable with meeting, greeting, and being touched by all types of people.
- **Go everywhere, do everything.** Try to find different buildings, floor surfaces, stairs, and elevators to introduce to your Shih Tzu. Take him on walks in areas that have more people, such as sidewalks in town, outdoor shopping malls, and outdoor cafes (that allow dogs).
- **Be groomed weekly.** The AAT dog must be washed within 24 hours of visiting the facility. It's a good idea to get him used to this now since you probably won't want to pay a groomer to bathe and blow dry your Shih Tzu once a week! Also, practice clipping nails and then using a large nail file to smooth the surfaces of the nails.
- **CGC certification.** ATT dogs must have a Canine Good Citizen Certificate.

Check with the Delta Society or Therapy Dog International (TDI) for a local organization (see "Useful Addresses and Literature"). Or, call your local shelters and obedience clubs for possible contact information.

A potential AAT Shih Tzu

- is at least one year old.
- enjoys being touched.
- is confident.
- is comfortable and curious in new situations and places.
- enjoys meeting new people of all shapes and sizes.
- is not particularly startled by loud noises and/or recovers quickly when he is startled.

Shih Tzu (and owners) of any age can get involved in AAT. Touchy, timid, or poorly socialized dogs are not suited to the job.

Canine Good Citizen

The Canine Good Citizen (CGC) certification was designed by the AKC as a sort of litmus test for good dogs and responsible pet owners. A Shih Tzu can take the test at any age, even as a young puppy. The test is pass/fail and involves ten separate mini tests, all of which must be passed to be certified.

The CGC requires some training to pass. Often, a training facility will offer testing for the CGC certification at the conclusion of a beginning obedience class. The CGC certification can be awarded to any Shih Tzu, regardless of whether or not he has AKC papers. Mixes may also test for the CGC certification. As noted previously,

Even young puppies may test for the Canine Good Citizen.

most AAT organizations require that a dog pass the CGC test in order to test for AAT certification.

CGC Tests

The following items are abbreviated summaries of the CGC test.

Test 1: Accepting a friendly stranger. In his first test, the Shih Tzu must stay by his handler's side as a friendly stranger walks up to the handler, shakes hands, and exchanges a few words. The Shih Tzu can't break from position (running over and doing Shih Tzu happy-crazies at the feet of the evaluator may bring a few smiles, but will fail the Shih Tzu), or behave in a fearful or aggressive manner.

Test 2: Sitting politely for petting. The friendly stranger reaches down to pet your Shih Tzu while he remains in a sit by your side. He can wiggle and wag his tail all he wants but must stay in the *sit*. Again, fear and aggression are big no-nos.

Test 3: Appearance and grooming. Bring your Shih Tzu's brush (and make sure he doesn't have any mats). In this exercise the evaluator will examine your Shih Tzu's ears and feet, and then run the brush through his coat.

Test 4: Out for a walk (walking on a loose lead). With your dog on-leash and at your side, you will be asked to walk a course that will include a right turn, a left turn, an about turn, and at least one halt. The dog isn't required to be perfect but he needs to walk nicely (without pulling) through the course.

Test 5: Walking through a crowd. The "crowd" you will need to walk through is a group of at least three people. Your Shih Tzu needs to walk nicely on his leash and not show any signs of over-exuberance, shyness, or resentment.

Test 6: *Sit* and *down* on command and *Stay in place*. You'll need to be able to demonstrate that you can put your Shih Tzu in a *sit* and *down* on command for this test. Then, you'll be asked to choose the *sit* or *down* to show that your Shih Tzu can perform a *stay*. While your dog is in a *stay*, you'll walk 20 feet away from your Shih Tzu (on a line) and then return to your dog.

Test 7: Coming when called. You'll put your Shih Tzu in a *sit* or *down-stay*, walk 10 feet from your dog, turn to face him, and call him to you. You will be able to use encouragement to get your dog to come if he hesitates.

Test 8: Reaction to another dog. You and your Shih Tzu will be required to approach another handler and dog, stop to shake hands and exchange a few words, and then walk on without your Shih Tzu showing more than casual interest in the other dog.

Test 9: Reaction to distraction. Two distractions will be presented to your Shih Tzu while with you and his reactions are evaluated. He is allowed to be curious or even slightly startled, but will fail the test if he panics, tries to run away, barks, or is aggressive. Distractions can include someone dropping a folding chair, jogging past the dog, or rolling a baby stroller.

Test 10: Supervised separation. The final test shows that your Shih Tzu will allow another person to take his leash while you go out of sight for three minutes.

A potential CGC Shih Tzu

■ is comfortable with people.
■ is comfortable with other dogs.
■ is neither fearful nor aggressive.
■ has learned (or is learning) *sit*, *down*, *stay*, and walks nicely on a leash

Training for the CGC can help take a Shih Tzu with a few rough edges and shape him into an excellent companion dog, so everyone and every dog should work toward this certification.

Conformation handling involves learning to groom your dog, as well as stacking him on the judge's table for examination.

Conformation

Dog showing is selecting today what will be the future of the breed tomorrow. Show dogs are not altered; the purpose is to find the Shih Tzu that most closely represent perfection in the breed as far as conformation, movement, and temperament, and award these outstanding individuals with championship points. When a Shih Tzu has received enough points (15 points with at least two major wins of three, four, or five points under two different judges), he is awarded his AKC Championship.

Judging is a very hands-on, involved process. Entries are initially divided by sex (males compete with males and females with females) and within each sex there are a variety of classes (puppy divisions,

Show dogs are trained to gait, or move in patterns, for the judge.

bred by exhibitor, open, etc.). If a dog wins in his individual class, he will be called back into the ring to be judged against the winners of the other classes within his sex. If he wins against other class winners, the Shih Tzu earns championship points according to how many other dogs he has beaten that day.

Your Shih Tzu will then compete against the winning opposite sex Shih Tzu for possibly more points and awards, and against seasoned Shih Tzu that hold AKC championships or "specials" for the title of Best of Breed.

As you might imagine, attaining a championship with a Shih Tzu is no small feat. As one of the most popular dogs in the country, show entries for the Shih Tzu are usually fairly large and yours will need to beat out a lot of other beautiful dogs to earn even a single point. If you plan on breeding your Shih Tzu, however, it is imperative that showing be part of your program.

Show Time!

Showing your Shih Tzu to his best advantage takes work and planning.

■ **Attend handling classes.** When competing against professional handlers (skilled handlers who make a living showing other people's dogs), an amateur handler must be polished, smooth, and confident. Make one mistake or a slip-up in the ring and it's almost assured that the judge will pass over your Shih Tzu, no matter how gorgeous he is. If you plan on handling your Shih Tzu, you will need to polish up your handling skills so that you and your Shih Tzu are ready for the ring. Handling classes are offered through all-breed clubs and are sometimes offered as private lessons by professionals.

■ **Secure a mentor for grooming.** The Shih Tzu is a coated breed, so it is important to work with an expert to properly learn how to bathe, dry, trim, and prepare your dog's coat (and that top knot) for the show ring.

■ **Socialize and acclimate.** The show dog is comfortable standing on a table as a complete stranger checks his teeth and runs hands all over him. Show dogs are also exposed to some of the craziest of situations. Noise, slick floors, rolling carts stacked with crates two to three high, and barking are all part of the show scene. Take your dog everywhere you can, travel frequently in the car, and get a dolly to roll his crate around in all sorts of places.

■ **Check your budget.** Showing a Shih Tzu is expensive. Entry fees are the smallest expense (roughly $25 to $30 per class) but factor in travel expenses, hotel, and incidentals. Even if the show is only a few hours away, it is quite easy to rack up $1,000 for a weekend. Hiring a professional handler to show your dog is even more expensive; however, because it usually takes an amateur much longer (i.e., more shows) to "finish" a dog (earn a championship),

the difference in total cost between hiring a handler and finishing a dog yourself may be nominal.

■ **Toughen up.** Judging is subjective. Every judge has his or her own personal interpretation of the breed standard and individual preferences. That's human nature. You could very well have a tremendous Shih Tzu, but some judges won't put your dog up for wins. That's okay. Everyone is in the same situation. If you have an outstanding Shih Tzu and you present him well, you'll be able to find judges who do like your Shih Tzu.

A potential show dog

■ **is impeccably bred.** Potential show Shih Tzu should have very few, if any, non-champions in the first three generations of his pedigree.

■ **is near perfect in conformation and movement.** We all love our dogs but just because you, your mom, or your best friend thinks, your Shih Tzu is gorgeous doesn't mean he's show quality. If you were sold your Shih Tzu on a show contract (requiring that your Shih Tzu be shown), your breeder will request photos and videos at specific ages to make sure your Shih Tzu is developing as he should and will be very honest with what you have (or don't have). If you didn't purchase your Shih Tzu as a show prospect (but you think he might be one), have an experienced breeder evaluate your Shih Tzu for you.

■ **has tremendous temperament.** There's no room for shy, timid, or surly dogs in the show ring. He must be bright, bold, and friendly.

- **loves the show ring.** You can have the whole package: good looks, a friendly disposition, and great health; but if your Shih Tzu doesn't want to strut, pose, and show off in the ring (he must "ask for the win"), he won't stand out enough to succeed.

Flyball

Flyball is a team sport that is popular in many areas of the country. The event is a relay race that involves four dog-and-handler teams. Each dog is sent out over a series of four low hurdles to a box. The box has a trigger that the dog pushes to make a ball pop out. The dog must catch the ball and run back over the hurdles to his handler.

If your Shih Tzu is nuts over balls, he might do well in flyball.

As soon as the first dog crosses back over the start line, the second dog sets off. When the fourth dog finishes, the time is recorded and the fastest team with the fewest faults wins.

It's a fun, fast-paced sport. Dogs are divided by height, so little guys—like the Shih Tzu—will not have to compete against bigger, faster breeds.

Getting Started

- **Get a health check.** There's a lot of high-speed running and jumping involved in flyball. Get a veterinary check to make sure everything is in working order so you don't accidentally exacerbate a pre-existing condition.
- **Speed up the recall.** The faster your Shih Tzu flies back to you, the more competitive he will be in this sport! When working on recalls, just before your Shih Tzu reaches you, turn around and run! He will go crazy chasing you. Make it fun and wild for him and he'll get it!
- **Encourage a healthy ball drive.** If your Shih Tzu is crazy about balls, help to foster this drive. Be careful never to overdo a fetch or play session; you don't want him to burn out and start ignoring balls.
- **Make it a group effort.** Find a flyball club or start your own. Contact the North American Flyball Association (see "Useful Addresses and Contacts").

The potential flyball Shih Tzu

- is ball crazy!
- has high energy and loves to run
- has no musculoskeletal issues
- is confident with other dogs

If you try your hand at formal obedience, the biggest competition will be with yourself. Relax and have fun!

Obedience

Formal obedience is a competitive activity in which dogs compete for titles. Companion Dog (CD) is the entry-level obedience title with the AKC. (The United Kennel Club also offers obedience competitions and titles.) Dogs and handlers enter the Novice classes to work towards a CD. Novice classes are divided into Novice A for inexperienced handlers and Novice B for handlers who have previously earned obedience titles.

For the CD, you and your dog will be scored on your ability to complete the following exercises: heel on lead and in a figure-eight, off-lead stand for exam-ination, heel off-lead, recall, *sit-stay* for one minute, and *down-stay* for three minutes.

To earn a CD title, you and your Shih Tzu must pass (earn 170 out of 200 possible points) three tests under three different judges. Once you've earned a CD title, you and your Shih Tzu can go on to work on higher levels: Companion Dog Excellent (CDX) and Utility Dog (UD).

Obedience is a competitive performance event. Handlers and their dogs not only earn titles for their efforts, but also receive placement awards for high scores. For example, a dog with 198 points may take first place in a Novice A division and High in Trial.

Upper level obedience requires retrieving a dumbbell over a jump.

dience dog because he can't be trained ad nauseum. It takes a creative handler with a lot of patience who isn't afraid of getting silly for his or her dog to keep the fun meter up at all times.

■ **Introduce dumbbells early.** If you want to achieve a CDX, your Shih Tzu will need to enjoy retrieving dumbbells. Introduce dumbbells as "special" fun toys that you throw out for games just as you would a ball.

Every Shih Tzu has the potential to earn the Companion Dog title, but those who excel

■ have high energy.
■ stay focused.
■ love to train.
■ learn quickly.

Obedience trials are only as competitive as you make them. If your goal is to earn a title and striving for a perfect score isn't your thing (or your Shih Tzu's), then that's fine. If you compete simply to see what score you can achieve, then you are your own competition. If you have an incredible obedience dog and a High in Trial is a possibility, go for it!

Getting Started

■ **Find a good obedience training club.** If you're going to be competitive, it's important to be able to practice in an environment that will be similar to the obedience ring.
■ **Keep up the excitement.**
■ **Rein in expectations.** The Shih Tzu is not known as a super-competitive obe-

Rally

Not quite ready for the obedience ring? Rally may be the perfect bridge into obedience trials—or the perfect sport for you and your Shih Tzu.

What makes rally-style obedience unique is that you are allowed to talk to your dog, praise him, and encourage him throughout the course.

Similar to a car rally where you go to each location and receive a different problem to solve or task to do, rally-style obedience has stations set up along a course with signs that indicate what you're supposed to do with your dog. For example, you could be asked to quicken or slow your pace, circle to the left or right, have your Shih Tzu go over a jump, or do an about turn or a figure-eight.

Three passing scores (70 out of 100) under two different judges are required for a title. Level I (Novice) is on-leash; Levels II and III (Advanced and Excellent) are off-leash.

Getting Started

Most obedience clubs offer a class in rally-style obedience. Usually you'll want to take a basic or beginning training class prior to participating in a rally-style obedience class.

Tracking

Believe it or not, Shih Tzu can track and they can earn titles, too!

Tracking requires that a dog follow a trail left by a person through various types of vegetation and terrain. Additionally, the tracking dog must indicate articles left on the track by the track layer.

The AKC offers three levels of tracking tests that are pass/fail and noncompetitive, as well as a tracking championship. Shih Tzu can compete and title in tracking; however, handlers need to take caution with weather conditions. Because the Shih Tzu is a brachycephalic breed, the dogs are at a disadvantage in hot temperatures and can overheat more quickly than long-nosed dogs.

To practice this sport, your Shih Tzu must maintain a short, clipped coat. A full coat could cause your Shih Tzu to become hung up or injured on the course.

The Shih Tzu's coat must be clipped to compete safely in tracking.

Getting Started

- **Find a tracking club.** This sport requires a team effort of track layers, trainers, and course designers. It also requires access to a large area of land.
- **Begin tracking skills early.** Puppies are great using their noses. If you don't encourage them to continue using their noses to track, sometimes they may shift to looking for things visually. Make little tracks in your home and backyard by dragging little bits of hot dog and leaving them along the trail to encourage good use of your Shih Tzu's sniffer!
- **Condition.** Tracking courses are long and can be over some rigorous terrain. Walk your Shih Tzu in the cool morning hours and build up to being able to walk for 30 to 45 minutes or more at a time. This sport requires that you be in condition, too.

The potential tracking Shih Tzu:

- is in good health and top physical fitness.
- possesses good scenting abilities.
- has an almost insatiable drive to find hidden toys and treats
- has a good energy level.

Useful Addresses and Literature

Organizations

American Kennel Club (AKC)
5580 Centerview Drive
Raleigh, NC 27606-3390
(919) 233-9767
www.akc.org

United Kennel Club (UKC)
100 East Kilgore Road
Kalamazoo, MI 49002-5584
(269) 343-9020
www.ukcdogs.com

American Shih Tzu Club, Inc.
279 Sun Valley Court
Ripon, CA 95366
www.shihtzu.org

Activities

Agility

American Kennel Club (AKC)
See "Organizations."

Canine Performance Events. Inc. (CPE)
P.O. Box 805
South Lyon, MI 48178
www.k9cpe.com

North American Dog Agility Council
 (NADAC)
P.O. Box 1206
Colbert, OK 74733
www.nadac.com

Teacup Dogs Agility Association
P. O. Box 158
Maroa, IL 61756
(217) 521-7955
www.k9tdaa.com

United Kennel Club (UKC)
See "Organizations."

United States Dog Agility Association
 (USDAA)
P.O. Box 850995
Richardson, TX 75085
(972) 487-2200
www.usdaa.com

Animal-assisted Therapy

The Delta Society
875 124th Ave. NE, Suite 101
Bellevue, WA 98005-2531
(425) 679-5500
www.deltasociety.org

Therapy Dogs International, Inc.
88 Bartley Road
Flanders, NJ 07836
(973) 252-9800
www.tdi-dog.org

R.E.A.D. (Reading Education Assistance
  Program)
Intermountain Therapy Animals
P.O. Box 17201
Salt Lake City, UT 84117
(801) 272-3439
www.therapyanimals.org/read

Behavior/Training

General

Animal Behavior Society
Indiana University
2611 East 10th Street
Bloomington, IN 47408-2603
(812) 856-5541
www.animalbehavior.org

American College of Veterinary
  Behaviorists (ACVB)
www.dacvb.org

American Veterinary Medical Association
1931 North Meacham Road, Suite 100
Schaumburg, IL 60173-4360
(847) 925-8070
www.avma.org

Association of Pet Dog Trainers (APDT)
150 Executive Center Drive, Box 35
Greenville, SC 29615
(800) PET-DOGS
www.apdt.com

International Association of
  Canine Professionals
P.O. Box 560156
Montverde, FL 34756-0156
(877) THE-IACP
www.dogpro.org

National Association of Dog Obedience
Instructors
PMB 369
729 Grapevine Highway
Hurst, TX 76054-2085
www.nadoi.org

Canine Good Citizen

See "Organizations."

Conformation

American Kennel Club
United Kennel Club
See "Organizations."

Flyball

North American Flyball Association (NAFA)
1400 West Devon Avenue, #512
Chicago, IL 60660
(800) 318-6312
www.flyball.org

Obedience

American Kennel Club
United Kennel Club
See "Organizations."

Rally

American Kennel Club
See "Organizations."

Association of Pet Dog Trainers
See "Behavior/Training."

Tracking

American Kennel Club
See "Organizations."

Books

Activities

Agility
Canova, Ali, Diane Goodspeed, Joe Canova, and Bruce Curtis. *Agility Training for You and Your Dog: From Backyard Fun to High-Performance Training.* Guilford, CT: Globe Pequot Press, 2008.
Simmons-Moake, Jane. *Agility Training, the Fun Sport for All Dogs.* New York: Howell Book House, 1992.
Simmons-Moake, Jane. *Excelling at Dog Agility: Book 1: Obstacle Training.* Houston, TX: Flashpaws Productions, 1999.

Animal-assisted Therapy
Burch, Mary R. *Wanted! Animal Volunteers.* New York: John Wiley & Sons, Inc., 2002.
Burch, Mary R. and Aaron Honori Katcher. *Volunteering with Your Pet: How to Get Involved in Animal-Assisted Therapy with Any Kind of Pet.* New York: John Wiley & Sons, Inc., 1996.

Howie, Ann R., Mary Burch, and Ellen Shay. *The Pet Partners Team Training Course: Pets Helping People Manual.* Seattle, WA: Delta Society, 2001.

Canine Good Citizen
Volhard, Jack, and Wendy Volhard. The *Canine Good Citizen: Every Dog Can Be One,* 2nd Edition. New York: John Wiley & Sons, Inc., 1997.

Conformation
Coile, Caroline D. *Show Me! A Dog Showing Primer,* 2nd Edition. Hauppauge, NY: Barron's Educational Series, Inc., 2009.
Ronchette, Vicki. *Positive Training for Show Dogs—Building a Relationship for Success.* Wenatchee, WA: Dogwise Publishing, 2007.
Smith, Cheryl S. *The Complete Guide to Showing Your Dog.* New York: Crown Publishing Group, 2001.

Flyball
Olson, Lonnie. *Flyball Racing: The Dog Sport for Everyone.* New York: John Wiley & Sons, Inc., 1997.
Parkin, Jacqueline. *Flyball Training—Start to Finish.* Crawford, CO: Alpine Publications, 1998.

Obedience
Anderson, Bobbie. *Building Blocks for Performance.* Crawford, CO: Alpine Publications, 2002.
Bauman, Diane L. *Beyond Basic Dog Training.* New York: John Wiley & Sons, 2003.

Spector, Morgan. *Clicker Training for Obedience: Shaping Top Performance Positively.* Waltham, MA: Sunshine Books, Inc., 1999.

Rally

Dearth, Janice. *The Rally Course Book: A Guide to AKC Rally Courses.* Crawford, CO: Alpine Publications, Inc., 2004.

Dennison, Pamela S. *Click Your Way to Rally Obedience.* Crawford, CO: Alpine Publications, Inc., 2006.

Kramer, Charles 'Bud.' *Rally-O: The Style of Rally Obedience,* 3rd Edition. Manhattan, KS: Fancee Publications, 2005.

Sawford, Marie. *Rally On.* Guelph, ON, Canada: Dog Sport Media, 2006.

Tracking

Krause, Carolyn. *Try Tracking! The Puppy Tracking Primer.* Wenatchee, WA: Dogwise Publishing, 2005.

Sanders, William 'Sil.' *Enthusiastic Tracking: A Step by Step Training Handbook.* Stanwood, WA: Rime Publications, 1998.

Behavior/Training

General Dog Behavior

Aloff, Brenda. *Canine Body Language, A Photographic Guide.* Wenatchee, WA: Dogwise Publishing, 2005.

Bailey, Jon S. and Mary R. Burch. *How Dogs Learn.* New York: John Wiley & Sons, Inc., 1999.

Coren, Stanley. *How Dogs Think: What the World Looks Like to Them and Why They Act the Way They Do.* New York: Simon & Schuster, 2005.

Coren, Stanley. *How to Speak Dog: Mastering the Art of Dog-Human Communication.* New York: Simon & Schuster, 2001.

Donaldson, Jean. *Oh Behave! Dogs from Pavlov to Premack to Pinker.* Wenatchee, WA: Dogwise Publishing, 2008.

Fogle, Bruce. *The Dog's Mind: Understanding Your Dog's Behavior.* New York: John Wiley & Sons, Inc., 1990.

McConnell, Patricia B. *The Other End of the Leash: Why We Do What We Do Around Dogs.* New York: Random House Publishing, 2003.

McConnell, Patricia B. *For the Love of a Dog: Understanding Emotion in You and Your Best Friend.* New York: Random House Publishing, 2006.

Problem Dog Behavior

Donaldson, Jean. *Mine! A Guide to Resource Guarding in Dogs.* San Francisco, CA: Kinship Communications/ SF-SPCA, 2002.

Killion, Jane. *When Pigs Fly: Training Success with Impossible Dogs.* Wenatchee, WA: Dogwise Publishing, 2007.

McConnell, Patricia B. *I'll Be Home Soon! How to Prevent and Treat Separation Anxiety.* Black Earth, WI: Dog's Best Friend, Ltd., 2000.

McConnell, Patricia B. *The Cautious Canine: How to Help Dogs Conquer Their Fears.* Black Earth, WI: Dog's Best Friend, Ltd., 1998.

McConnell, Patricia B. and Karen B. London. *The Feisty Fido: Help for the Leash-Aggressive Dog.* Black Earth, WI: Dog's Best Friend, Ltd., 2003.

Pryor, Karen. *Don't Shoot the Dog! The New Art of Teaching and Training.* Waltham, MA: Sunshine Books, Inc., 2006.

Rugass, Turid. *Barking: The Sound of a Language.* Wenatchee, WA: Dogwise Publishing, 2008.

Rugass, Turid. *My Dog Pulls. What Do I Do?* Wenatchee, WA: Dogwise Publishing, 2005.

Clicker Training

Book, Mandy and Cheryl Smith. *Quick Clicks: 40 Fast and Fun Behaviors to Train with a Clicker.* Wenatchee, WA: Dogwise Publishing, 2001.

Pryor, Karen. *Click! Dog Training System.* New York: Metro Books, 2007.

Pryor, Karen. *Clicker Training for Dogs,* 4th Edition. Waltham, MA: Sunshine Books, Inc., 2005.

Head Halter Training

Fields-Babineau, Miriam. *Dog Training with a Head Halter.* Hauppauge, NY: Barron's Educational Series, Inc., 2000.

House-training

Kalstone, Shirlee. *How to Housebreak Your Dog in 7 Days,* 2nd Edition. New York: Bantam Books, 2004.

Palika, Liz. *The Pocket Idiot's Guide to Housetraining Your Dog.* New York: Penquin Group (USA), 2007.

Socializing with Dogs

Bennett, Robin and Susan Briggs. *Off-leash Dog Play: A Complete Guide to Safety and Fun.* Woodbridge, VA: C&R Publishing, LLC, 2008.

McConnell, Patricia B. *Feeling Outnumbered? How to Manage and Enjoy Your Multi-dog Household* (expanded and updated edition). Black Earth, WI: Dog's Best Friend, Ltd., 2008.

Socializing with People

Long, Lorie. *A Dog Who's Always Welcome: Assistance and Therapy Dog Trainers Teach You How to Socialize and Train Your Companion Dog.* New York: John Wiley & Sons, Inc., 2008.

McConnell, Patricia B. *How to Be the Leader of the Pack and Have Your Dog Love You for It!* Black Earth, WI: Dog's Best Friend, Limited, 1996.

Trick Training

Haggerty, Captain and Arthur J. Haggerty. *How to Teach Your Dog to Talk: 125 Easy-to-Learn Tricks Guaranteed to Entertain Both You and Your Pet.* New York: Simon & Schuster: 2000.

Sundance, Kyra. *101 Dog Tricks: Step-by-Step Activities to Engage, Challenge and Bond with Your Dog.* Bloomington, IN: Quarry Books, 2007.

Index

Playmates, 48–49
Positive reinforcement, 15–16
Praise, 18, 30, 59
Primary reinforcement, 72–73
Public transportation, 126–127
Puppy
age of, 13, 46
bringing home, 52–53
early environments for, 57–58
learning by, 11–15
littermates of, 46
places to avoid, 47–48
playmates of, 48–49
reactions to noise, 56–59, 62–63
socialization of. See Socialization
Purebred alternative listing, 129

R
Rally, 138–139, 142
Reactions, 56–59
Recall, 112, 136
Reinforcements, 72–74
Relaxation, 63
Repeating of commands, 93
Repetition, 74–75
Rescue dogs, 40, 64
Retractable leashes, 71
Rewards, 16–19, 61
Rules, 37–38

S
Safety, 34–36, 47, 63
Schedule, 24–26

Secondary reinforcement, 73–74
Second dogs, 52–53
Senses, 56
Separation anxiety, 64–65
Sexual maturity, 14
Show dogs, 134–136
Side-by-side walking, 49, 53
Sit, 10, 82–85, 93, 112–113, 132
Sit-stay, 86, 88, 91, 112–113
Slip collars, 70
Smell sense, 56
Smiling, 42–43
Socialization
of adult dog, 40
body language during, 42–43
at home, 32–33
need for, 32
off-leash, 35
on-leash, 37–39
quantity of, 33–34
safety in, 47
of show dog, 135
Space, 20–22
Speak, 110
Stand, 100–101
Stand-stay, 101–102
Stay, 86–88
Stressed body language, 43

T
Tail droop, 43
Take it, 103–105
Teeth, 67
Temperament, 44–45, 56, 135
Thunderstorms, 62–63
Timidity, 58
Timing, 22–24, 30, 80–81

Tracking, 139
Training
advantages of, 1–3
challenges of, 4–7
reasons for, 1–8
when not to train, 75–76
Training clubs, 76–77
Training programs, 77
Travel
airline, 124–125
car, 119–122
carrier for, 116–118, 120
public transportation, 126–127
skills for, 122–124
wait command, 118–119
Treats, 5, 38, 78–79, 117
Turnaround, 125

U
Urine spots, 27

V
Vaccinations, 34
Verbal comprehension, 11
Veterinarian, 63
Veterinarian's office, 47
Vision, 56
Visual learning, 9–10

W
Wait, 118–119
Walk nicely, 91–92
Walks
come during, 89–91
on leash, 132
side-by-side, 49, 53
Water bottle, 123–124

Y
Yawning, 43